IMAGES
of America

OCEANSIDE POLICE DEPARTMENT

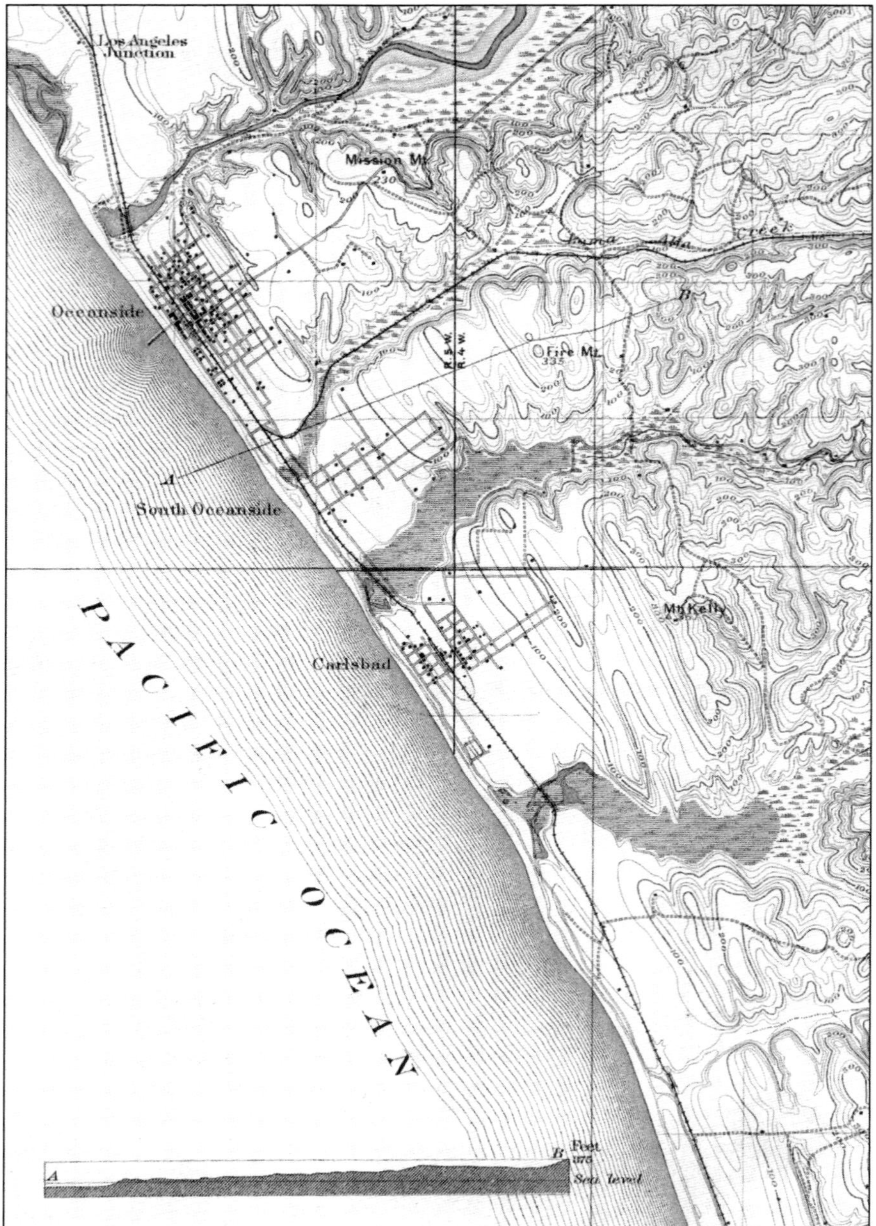

This map depicts Oceanside, which was incorporated in 1888, along with South Oceanside, Carlsbad, and San Luis Rey, as they were during the early 1900s. Oceanside, located 35 miles north of the City of San Diego, eventually absorbed the townships of South Oceanside, San Luis Rey, and a portion of Carlsbad and became the largest populated city in north San Diego County, encompassing 42 square miles. Much of the area between the towns depicted on this map was still rugged and undeveloped. (Courtesy Matthew J. Lyons.)

ON THE COVER: In this 1954 photograph, chief of police Edwin W. Patrick, along with his 3 captains, 4 sergeants, 3 detectives, 3 secretaries, and 15 patrolmen, form up behind the old police station, located at 305 North Nevada Street. (Courtesy Capt. H. B. Davis family.)

IMAGES
of America

OCEANSIDE POLICE DEPARTMENT

Matthew J. Lyons

ARCADIA
PUBLISHING

ISBN 978-0-7385-3112-0

Published by Arcadia Publishing
Charleston, South Carolina

Printed in the United States of America

Library of Congress Catalog Card Number: 2005937816

For all general information contact Arcadia Publishing at:
Telephone 843-853-2070
Fax 843-853-0044
E-mail sales@arcadiapublishing.com
For customer service and orders:
Toll-Free 1-888-313-2665

Visit us on the Internet at www.arcadiapublishing.com

I would like to dedicate this book to the men and women who have served in the past and currently wear the uniforms of their respective communities, making this country a safer place. Additionally, I would like to further dedicate this effort to Oceanside's fallen lawmen: City Marshal Charles C. Wilson, End of Watch (EOW) July 4, 1889; City Marshal John E. Mugan, EOW September 24, 1916; and my friend, Ofc. Tony W. Zeppetella, EOW June 13, 2003. I further release all royalties that I would have gained from the sale of this book to be donated to the National Law Enforcement Officers Memorial Fund (NLEOMF), whose mission is to generate increased public support for the law enforcement profession by permanently recording and appropriately commemorating the service and sacrifice of law enforcement officers, and to provide information that will help promote law enforcement safety. For more information, please visit nleomf.com.

CONTENTS

ACKNOWLEDGMENTS

No project like this could ever become reality without the time, dedication, and foresight of many people over the years to preserve and document the history of the Oceanside Police Department. This book is the result of efforts by many people who came before me, took the time to make notes, set aside old photographs, and add valuable tidbits of information to them. It is that spirit and sense of history, along with the desire to provide a window into the history of the local police department, that allows projects like this to become reality. It is not possible to fully recognize all those involved over the years, and any omission of persons is purely unintentional. So with that said, I would like to mention the following persons or groups who I have relied upon for assistance to guide me through this process. The first person to recognize is retired police captain Harold B. Davis, now deceased. If it were not for Captain Davis's tireless and meticulous work to set aside artifacts and vital information from the early years of this police department, much of this book would not have come to be. So I thank his family for allowing me a personal look into their family collection. Further, I would like to include, but not exclusively, Sgts. Kevin Kaiser and Dan Shapiro and Mr. Nathan Semel, whose volunteer work as Oceanside Police Department historians have been invaluable to both this project and the overall preservation of Oceanside police history. Also, I would like to thank Steve Willard of the San Diego Police Historical Association for his contributions that helped to blaze the way for this book, following his own; Kristi Hawthorne of the City of Oceanside Historical Society, whose passion to preserve and help others preserve history goes beyond the call of duty; and the leadership of the *North County Times* for allowing the use of old articles. I need to acknowledge the families of those officers who have served. Their sacrifices are many! Lastly I would like to thank my wife, Cindy, and our three children, who have been supportive of me while working on this project and countless others.

INTRODUCTION

Acclaimed artist Norman Rockwell's painting entitled *Runaway* features a police officer sitting on a stool beside a young boy inside an old greasy spoon diner. A cook is across the counter from them, listening in. The police officer is speaking with the boy, who is apparently running away from home. Rockwell does an excellent job of capturing the authority and compassion of the police officer and the innocence of the boy and the scene. Much like this image, I hope this book is able to capture those same sentiments and allow the reader to go back in time to see the proud history of the Oceanside Police Department, along with people who have made up the rank and file.

To understand the Oceanside Police Department, one must go back to the time when Oceanside was just beginning. The town of Oceanside was formed in the late 1800s in the northerly portion of the San Diego County coast. The famous Mission San Luis Rey is located seven miles east of this location along with the smaller town of San Luis Rey.

In the early 1880s, a town marshal and constables policed Oceanside. The primary job of the constables was to transport prisoners to San Diego for trial. Constables were paid $2 per prisoner. The town marshal had the added task of tax collection, along with the sale and seizure of property when so ordered by the local justice of the peace. Oceanside's town jail, made of two-by-four timbers, was rumored to be standing room only on some weekends, with about 20 square feet of space.

Many early pioneers came to the area from all parts to settle in this new frontier. One of those pioneers was Charles Clinton Wilson, known by his friends as C. C. Wilson. Wilson, who was born in Visalia, California, moved to Texas with his family as a boy and would later serve briefly as a Texas Ranger. He eventually returned to California as one of the early pioneers of Oceanside.

In 1888, Oceanside incorporated as a city with a population of 1,000, and the city trustees appointed C. C. Wilson as the first city marshal. The city marshal and his constables worked out of a tiny office on the second floor of the Oceanside Bank and City Hall building.

Almost a year to the date of his appointment, Wilson would also become the city's first fallen officer when a drunken cowboy from San Luis Rey, John Murray, shot the marshal down in cold blood while resisting arrest.

The city of Oceanside was a community that was growing fast, with a train station that connected Los Angeles to San Diego, emerging commerce, and recreation. A pier had been built along with a grand hotel to accommodate the tourism.

In 1893, a sheet-metal jail, located in the 100 block of Cleveland, served the city. It was later replaced with a concrete structure around 1905. This structure was saved from destruction during the 1980s and is currently on display in the city's Heritage Park.

The city recorded its first armed robbery in September 1905, when a doorman at a local opera house was robbed of $10 in quarters by subjects unknown. The case was never solved.

This increase of crime may have led to the next Oceanside first—the establishment of a formal Department of Police in 1906, via Ordinance No. 171. This new law outlined improvements for protection and appointed G. D. Love as a special policeman, who would more closely monitor those who were passing through the city.

It would not be until 1925 that the titles of city marshal and constable marshal would change to chief of police and patrolman. During this time, Charles Goss, a former city marshal, was appointed the first chief of police. Goss, like many of the chiefs who followed him, would oversee a department of dedicated individuals, committed to serving their community.

In 1925, officers moved out of the Oceanside Bank building, even though no official police facility existed. Ofcs. Ed Hall and Fred Sickler, who assisted Chief Goss, would go to an Oceanside garage, located at what is now the 200 block of Coast Highway, where calls for police assistance were received. Ofc. Ed Hall used his own 1924 Model T Ford to transport the prisoners to San Diego.

Highway 101, which runs directly through the heart of the city, was both a benefit for tourism for the young city and also a problem for the police, due to the increase in traffic. In 1927, Warren Paxton, who would later go on to become chief of police, was hired as a motorcycle officer and paid $135 a month. Paxton furnished his own cycle, fuel, and tires.

In 1929, the Oceanside Police Department had three full-time officers. Harold B. Davis, hired as the fourth full-time officer in 1930, worked the night shift, using his own 1930 Model A Ford to patrol the city. Davis was also appointed a San Diego County deputy sheriff and was required to patrol and police the nearby city of Carlsbad. When he retired as a police captain in 1955, Davis would become the first full-time officer to receive a full pension from the city for his 25 years of service. Upon his retirement, the citizens of Oceanside pitched in and bought Davis a brand new 1955 Chevy Bel Air sedan.

It was not until 1932 that the city built a police and fire complex, located at the intersection of Pierview and Nevada Streets. A booking officer was hired and doubled as a fireman. The new police facility also provided space for the recently formed California Highway Patrol (CHP), where it remained until 1954.

With the stock market crash in 1929, the Depression brought many jobseekers West by railroad, but few jobs were available. The duties of the police included rounding up local "hobos and tramps" for morning and evening meals that were provided by local businesses.

In 1933, police communication was improved when a red light was attached to a tall pole atop the police station. When a call for service came in, the chief's secretary, Mary Todd—who later became the first Oceanside woman police officer—would flip the red light on. When officers saw the light on, they returned to the station.

Also in 1933, Oceanside installed its first patrol car radios when a local citizen built a radio transmitter at his shop and installed one in a police car. This would change in 1935, when a more improved radio transmitter was built and installed at the police station and in the police cars. The Oceanside Police Department is believed to be the fifth city in the nation to have radios in the police cars.

In 1935, Oceanside police officers were issued new standardized blue uniforms and police badges. The California Pacific International Fair was being held in San Diego, and the city wanted to project a more professional and appealing image. From 1937 through 1940, Oceanside created its first fingerprinting and criminal identification files.

In 1940, the department was 12 officers strong, including the chief. In 1943, the department grew to 16 officers under the leadership of Chief William Coyle. With the recent purchase of the Santa Margarita ranch by the military to build Marine Corps Training Base Camp Pendleton, the need for increased assistance or manpower existed. The Marine Corps Military Police (MPs) supplemented patrols, partnering with Oceanside police officers. The old jail on Cleveland was turned over to the MPs to use as a police station. This jail was used by the MPs until 1955, when they began using their own facility at Cleveland and Michigan. The MPs would continue to patrol Oceanside city streets until 1978.

In 1950, all members of the police department began wearing the new tan uniforms. The blue style was deemed no longer fashionable after 45 years in Southern California.

In February 1951, Oceanside began using a new scientific device called the Intoximeter to accurately measure alcohol intoxication. In 1953, the department had grown to 27 male officers and 3 policewomen. In January 1954, the Police Reserve Program was restarted. It originally began as the Civil Defense Auxiliary and at one point numbered 46 police reserve officers. In 1962, the police department grew to 42 regular officers. Also in 1962, Oceanside's first woman police officer, Mary Todd, retired after 30 years of service.

During the early 1960s, the Oceanside Police Department stayed in step with other major California jurisdictions, increasing professionalism by requiring all new officers to attend a formal training academy before becoming officers. Up to that point, no formal training was required.

With the increase of racial militants and radical dissidents in society, new equipment and rules were implemented. These rules required that all police cars be fitted with protective cages separating the front and back seats, and officers were required to wear safety helmets (now called riot helmets).

The need for a bigger facility resulted in a move from the police station on Nevada Street. On February 29, 1968, the police department moved to a larger station located at Mission Avenue and Barnes. Through the 1960s and 1970s, tensions increased with the controversial Vietnam War, causing added problems for the police department. In 1973, three canine patrols were added to the force to aid hostile crowd control. By the mid-1970s, the department grew to 92 officers. However, violent crime had increased by 63 percent the previous year. Crime would rise and fall over the next 32 years, leveling out during the late 1990s.

Oceanside has lost three officers in the line of duty—City Marshal Charles C. Wilson in 1889, City Marshal John E. Mugan in 1916, and Ofc. Tony W. Zeppetella in 2003. Each of these officers, like all who have taken a sworn oath to be willing to stand on that symbolic thin blue line between evil and good, served Oceanside with distinction. Their sacrifices are not forgotten. And they remain a torch of righteousness, lighting the way for those who continue their mission after them. Today the Oceanside Police Department includes 195 sworn officers, 102 professional staff members, and more than 100 civilian and retired volunteers. In 2006, the Oceanside Police Department celebrates its centennial.

Delores Davis Sloan is pictured here as a young girl in 1950 with her father, Captain H. B. Davis. They rode together in the Days of San Luis Rey Fiesta parade and won a third prize and guest-of-honor ribbon as a team. It is because of Delores's generosity and sharing of historic artifacts and images that this book came to be. (Courtesy Capt. H. B. Davis family.)

One

The City Marshal's Office and the Department of Police 1888–1920s

This six-point star is a replica of an original Oceanside series No. 1 badge worn by City Marshal J. Keno Wilson during his time as a lawman in Oceanside. It was a one-of-a-kind badge that dates back to the late 1880s and is considered the oldest badge still in existence in San Diego County. Lawmen were required to purchase their own equipment, which included the badge they wore. The original badge is on display in the San Diego History Museum in Balboa Park, San Diego. J. Keno Wilson started his career in Oceanside as a constable deputy marshal in 1888 at age 21, working under his brother, then City Marshal Charles Clinton Wilson. Keno would later become city marshal after he watched his brother's murder by San Luis Rey cowboy John Murray in the street near the St. Cloud Hotel, which no longer exists at the corner of Pierview Way and Cleveland Street. (Courtesy Matthew J. Lyons.)

Jefferson Keno Wilson was chief of the San Diego Police Department. Keno was born on October 26, 1862, one of 12 children, in Visalia, California. He worked for his brother Charlie as an Oceanside deputy city marshal and eventually became the city marshal, after he watched his older sibling die in the line of duty. Keno remained in Oceanside until 1893, when he was appointed a San Diego County deputy sheriff. He remained as a deputy sheriff until 1895 when he became a line rider for the U.S. Customs Service, patrolling the California and Arizona borders. In 1899, Keno left the Customs Service on December 18, joining the SDPD. On May 3, 1909, he was appointed chief of police, and he retired on May 17, 1926. Upon retiring, he became a deputy U.S. marshal for the San Diego area until 1933, when he fully retired. Keno Wilson died in San Diego on September 24, 1934, at the age of 71. (Courtesy San Diego Police Historical Association.)

POLICE
MEMBER NATIONAL BUREAU OF IDENTIFICATION

POLICE DEPARTMENT

City of San Diego, California

BRUNO HESTER

Age 33 years. Height 5 ft. 11 ins. Weight 175 pounds. Hair light brown, slightly bald on top. Eyes blue. Complexion light.

DESCRIPTION

Large prominent scar on forehead, may be covered up when hair is combed. Large cowlick back of head. Medium large stomach. Short broad hands. Pop-eyed. Musician by profession, plays cornet mostly, belongs to the Musician's Union of this City. Is a gambler and plays for big money.

Hester induced a man by the name of E. C. Moore to draw $3,500 from the bank with the understanding that they would double-cross a third party and get his money. This occurred on Sept. 14, 1912. On Oct. 8, 1912, E. C. Moore's body was found weighted down with 500 lbs. of iron, in the San Diego bay. Hester taking the train north on the 16th of September, 1912, and has not been heard from since.

We hold warrant charging this man with murder. If located arrest, hold and wire at my expense, and I will send officer at once with proper papers.

We understand this man Hester is in your vicinity.

J. K. WILSON, Chief of Police.

November 20, 1912.

This wanted poster was published on November 20, 1912, by former Oceanside city marshal J. Keno Wilson, three years after he was appointed as the chief of the San Diego Police Department. Chief Wilson and his department were investigating a homicide in San Diego and looking for Bruno Hester, who allegedly murdered a man for $3,500 and dumped the victim's body in San Diego Bay, with 500 pounds of weight attached to it. Wanted posters, or "old handbills," as they were called, originally were made popular in old Westerns. They were used as early as the 19th century and sometimes offered a reward for the capture of the wanted person. The use of wanted posters has remained an important lawman's tool. (Courtesy Matthew J. Lyons.)

This vintage postcard depicts how the city would have appeared to early lawmen. It portrays Oceanside during the early 1900s, with a view looking east onto Second Street (now Mission Avenue) from Cleveland. The horse and wagons pictured show the mode of transportation for the city marshals who patrolled the city. The choices were either by foot, wagon, or horseback. On a summer day, the streets were dusty with the ocean breeze kicking up the loose soil and

smells of livestock and animal waste in the streets. The tall clock tower of the city hall and city marshal's office are visible in the distance, located at the northwest corner of the intersection of Second Street (now Mission Avenue) and Hill Street (now Coast Highway or Highway 101). (Courtesy Matthew J. Lyons.)

Before San Luis Rey became part of Oceanside, it was a township, even before Oceanside was founded. During the 1880s, San Luis Rey Township, located near the famous Mission San Luis Rey, consisted of a hotel, a post office, a general store, and a newspaper. Ben Hubbert, pictured here, was a rancher in the San Luis Rey Valley and would later become the lawman for the area. Hubbert, appointed constable in 1902, would become a deputy sheriff for San Diego County in the Oceanside area in 1907. Constable Hubbert, on horseback, was said to have declined an offer for a new Model T automobile, explaining it was easier for him to ford the dry riverbed of the San Luis Rey River with a horse when traveling from his home into town. By all accounts, Constable Hubbert was a firm but fair man and was respected by the local residents. (Courtesy Oceanside Historical Society.)

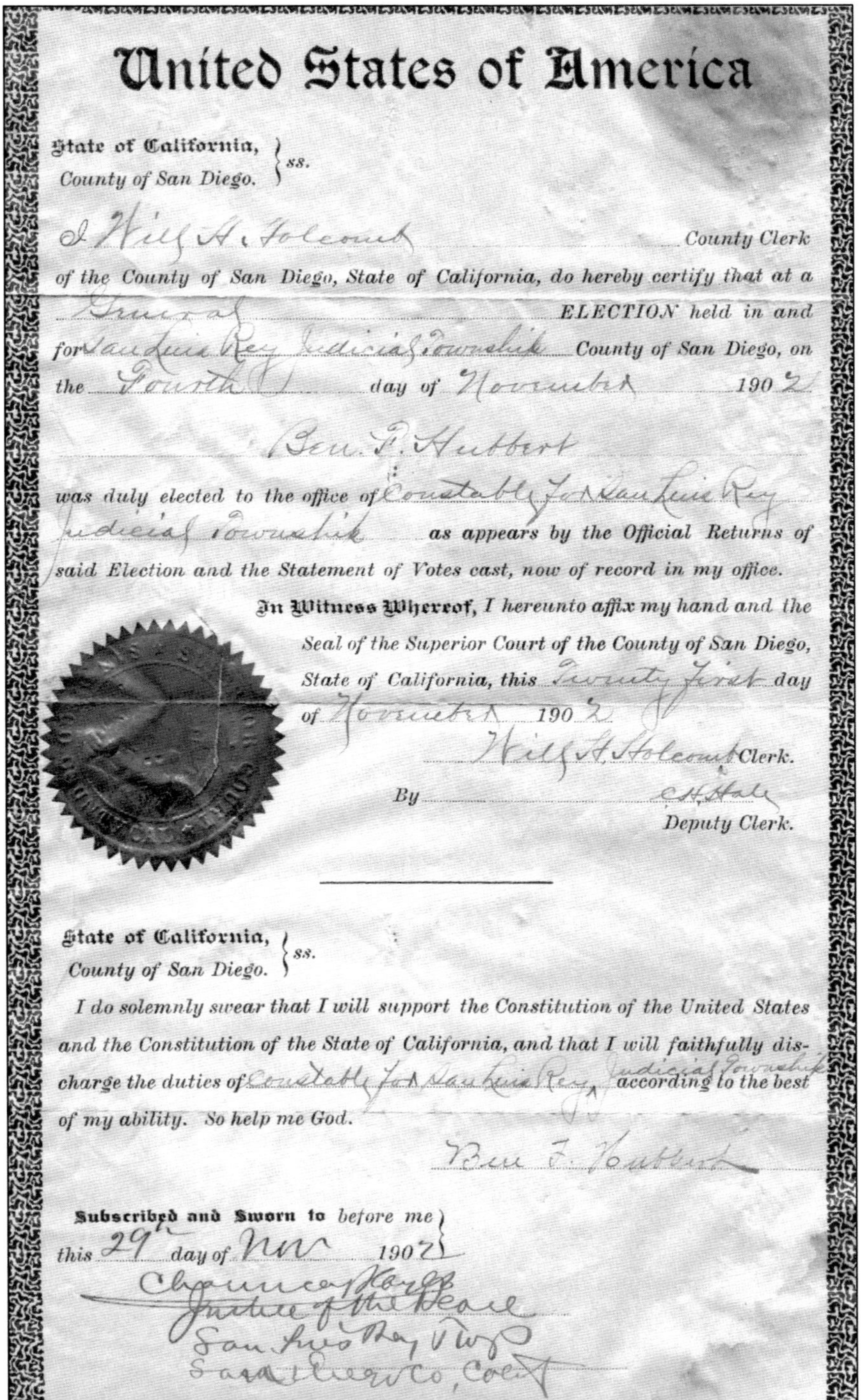
United States of America

State of California, }
County of San Diego. } ss.

I Will H. Holcourt County Clerk of the County of San Diego, State of California, do hereby certify that at a General ELECTION held in and for San Luis Rey Judicial Township County of San Diego, on the Fourth (4) day of November 1902

Ben F. Hubbert

was duly elected to the office of Constable for San Luis Rey Judicial Township as appears by the Official Returns of said Election and the Statement of Votes cast, now of record in my office.

In Witness Whereof, I hereunto affix my hand and the Seal of the Superior Court of the County of San Diego, State of California, this Twenty First day of November 1902

Will H. Holcourt Clerk.

By C. H. Hale
Deputy Clerk.

State of California, }
County of San Diego. } ss.

I do solemnly swear that I will support the Constitution of the United States and the Constitution of the State of California, and that I will faithfully discharge the duties of Constable for San Luis Rey Judicial Township according to the best of my ability. So help me God.

Ben F. Hubbert

Subscribed and Sworn to before me this 29th day of Nov 1902

Chauncey Hayes
Justice of the Peace
San Luis Rey Twp
San Diego Co, Cal

This original certificate reflects that on November 4, 1902, Ben F. Hubbert was duly elected by general election to the office of constable for San Luis Rey Judicial Township. Superior Court clerk Will H. Holcourt, of San Diego County, verified the official election returns on November 21, 1902. Justice of the peace of San Luis Rey Township, Chauncey Hayes, swore Hubbert into office on November 29, 1902. (Courtesy Capt. H. B. Davis family.)

As most who ride a horse know, equipment is everything. San Luis Rey constable Ben Hubbert knew this as well, first as a rancher and later as a lawman, where his primary means of transportation was his horse. These are the original spurs owned and used by Hubbert. Ben would hang them on his saddle horn after tying his horse to a hitching post before entering the local café to get a cup of coffee. These spurs date back to the 1800s and were most likely made at a local blacksmith, perhaps at the nearby Mission San Luis Rey, which had a fully functioning blacksmith on-site. (Courtesy Capt. H. B. Davis family.)

Justice of the peace Chauncey Hayes, the son of a district judge, came to San Luis Rey first and would later help develop the downtown area. As a real estate agent, he made the application for a post office and submitted the name Oceanside. He also worked as a lawyer, farmer, and editor of a local newspaper, along with his duties as justice of the peace, which included swearing local lawmen into office and hearing minor criminal cases. (Courtesy Oceanside Historical Society.)

This police shield is a replica of an original Oceanside series No. 2-style badge, which would have been worn by City Marshal John Mugan and others during the early 1900s. It was relatively cheap in price and since lawman bought their own, it was a common style. Mugan, killed in 1916 by Patrick Burke in front of Trotter and Hosp Billiard Hall, had been a deputy sheriff in Tonopah, Nevada, and the under-sheriff of Las Vegas, Nevada, for many years before coming to Oceanside to work as a city marshal. (Courtesy Matthew J. Lyons.)

This vintage postcard depicts how the famous San Luis Rey Mission, founded in 1798, appeared during 1901, located adjacent to the township named after it. The mission, called the "King of the Missions" because of its size, covered six acres and was surrounded by 200,000 acres of farmland. The mission is located today near the intersection of Mission Avenue and Rancho Del Oro. City Marshal John Mugan was buried there in 1916 after he was killed in the line of duty. (Courtesy Matthew J. Lyons.)

City marshal from 1917 to 1922, Patrolman Fred Sickler, pictured here in 1937, was a longtime Oceanside resident and lawman. Before that, he had been a U.S. deputy marshal. Sickler, who had a law school background, worked in law enforcement for over 30 years and was considered a legal authority by many who knew him. (Courtesy Capt. H. B. Davis family.)

With the increase of tourism to Oceanside in 1887, the South Pacific Hotel, which is no longer standing, was built. It was located at what is now Pacific Street and Pierview Way (Third Street). On July 4, 1889, the hotel was to be the place of a grand Independence Day celebration. Instead it became a memorial site for City Marshal Charles C. Wilson, who was killed in the line of duty on the same day during the early morning hours when he attempted to arrest a drunken cowboy. (Courtesy Oceanside Historical Society.)

This 1925 photograph shows Charles Goss when he was chief of the Oceanside Police Department. Seen wearing his signature sport coat and fedora, Goss struck a strong figure and was clearly a man of business. Goss had been the Oceanside city marshal from 1922 until 1925, when he became the first chief of police. Described as a man of upright and forceful character in the September 1931 issue of the *California Police Journal*, Goss was credited with totally abolishing crime during his tenure. According to this article, Goss "has upheld the rights of the law-abiding citizens continually, and driven habitual hoodlums from the city." Goss was also credited with taking Patrick Burke, the murderer of City Marshal John Mugan (Oceanside's second fallen officer), into custody in 1916 as they stood outside the Trotter and Hosp Billiard Hall. (Courtesy Capt. H. B. Davis family.)

Ofc. Warren Paxton, pictured here as a young new officer, was the third man hired by Chief Charles Goss in 1927. He later became the first traffic officer and supplied his own motorcycle. He was paid $135 a month when he began. He also later became the third police chief, serving from 1936 to 1943. Under his leadership, many improvements were made, including a two-way radio system and international fingerprint checkup system, along with other scientific equipment that included a ballistics testing chamber. Chief Paxton was born in 1901 and died unexpectedly in 1943 from a severe case of pneumonia while visiting his parents in Minnesota. (Courtesy Capt. H. B. Davis family.)

Two

People and Places of the OPD

1930s, 1940s, and 1950s

Edward Hall proudly stands in his makeshift uniform outside his home on November 23, 1930, with an unidentified woman. As illustrated in this photograph, police uniforms were whatever the officer could put together that might look official. Many times military uniforms or truck driving uniforms were coordinated together to create a uniform. Ed Hall was originally hired by City Marshal Charles Goss in 1922 as a deputy constable and later became a policeman in 1925, when Goss was appointed as chief of police. Hall lived at 120 South Cleveland near the old city jail and was an officer until 1934, serving only four years. Hall died in 1954. (Courtesy Capt. H. B. Davis family.)

In 1933, Harold Davis stands proudly in uniform. Davis was first hired in 1929 as a special officer to work the local dances on weekends; however, he was later hired on full time, the fourth man in the department. His hat was an old truck driver's hat; his trousers were old Marine Corps officers' breeches. At night, he patrolled Oceanside and Carlsbad in his own 1930 Model A, with one red light attached to the left fender. (Courtesy Capt. H. B. Davis family.)

This Western Union telegram was the only way Ofc. Harold B. Davis's dad could relay a message to Harold in South Dakota that Chief Charles Goss had hired him as a full-time officer. The message, dated November 11, 1932, reads, "Goss says you can start work as soon as you arrive." (Courtesy Capt. H. B. Davis family.)

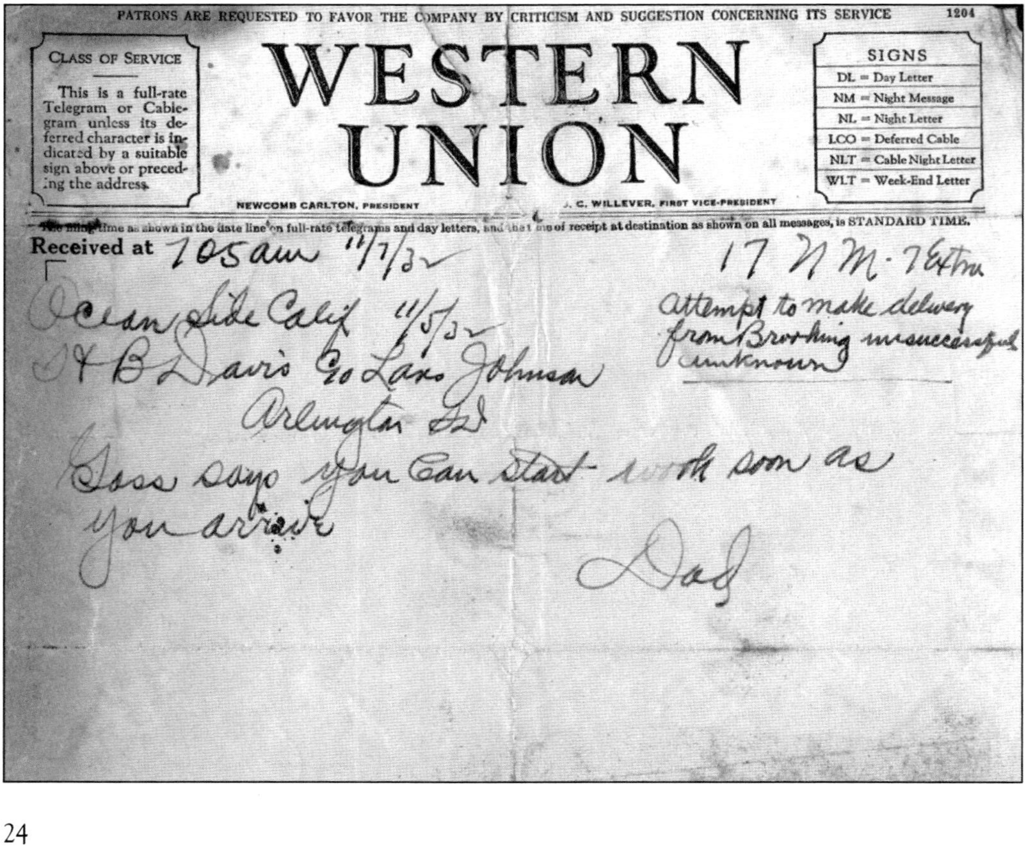

PATRONS ARE REQUESTED TO FAVOR THE COMPANY BY CRITICISM AND SUGGESTION CONCERNING ITS SERVICE 1204

CLASS OF SERVICE

This is a full-rate Telegram or Cablegram unless its deferred character is indicated by a suitable sign above or preceding the address.

WESTERN UNION

NEWCOMB CARLTON, PRESIDENT J. C. WILLEVER, FIRST VICE-PRESIDENT

SIGNS

DL = Day Letter
NM = Night Message
NL = Night Letter
LCO = Deferred Cable
NLT = Cable Night Letter
WLT = Week-End Letter

The filing time as shown in the date line on full-rate telegrams and day letters, and the time of receipt at destination as shown on all messages, is STANDARD TIME.

Received at 7 05 am 11/7/32 17 NM · 7 Extra

Ocean Side Calif 11/5/32

H B Davis Co Lars Johnson

Arlington SD

Goss says you can start work soon as you arrive

Dad

attempt to make delivery from Brookings unsuccessful unknown

Ofc. Bill Jensen with the California Highway Patrol (CHP) is pictured here in 1932, reenacting the position he held behind a telephone pole during a shootout with a subject wanted in an earlier shooting in Carlsbad, California. The fallen suspect can be seen in the distance, covered by a blanket and surrounded by a crowd. CHP had recently been created and had an office at the Oceanside Police Department, located at the corner of Nevada and Third Streets. Jensen worked closely with Oceanside officer H. B. Davis, who also responded to this Officer Involved Shooting (OIS) call. (Courtesy Capt. H. B. Davis family.)

This 1932 photograph is the view seen by Ofc. H. B. Davis as he held a position of partial cover and concealment from behind the right rear fender of his 1930 Model A patrol car during a shootout with a suspect. Officer Davis had responded, with CHP officer Bill Jensen, to Carlsbad concerning a report of a shooting at a local meat market by a suspect with a rifle who was angry over a $40 bill. The fallen suspect is seen in the distance, with a large crowd surrounding the body. (Courtesy Capt. H. B. Davis family.)

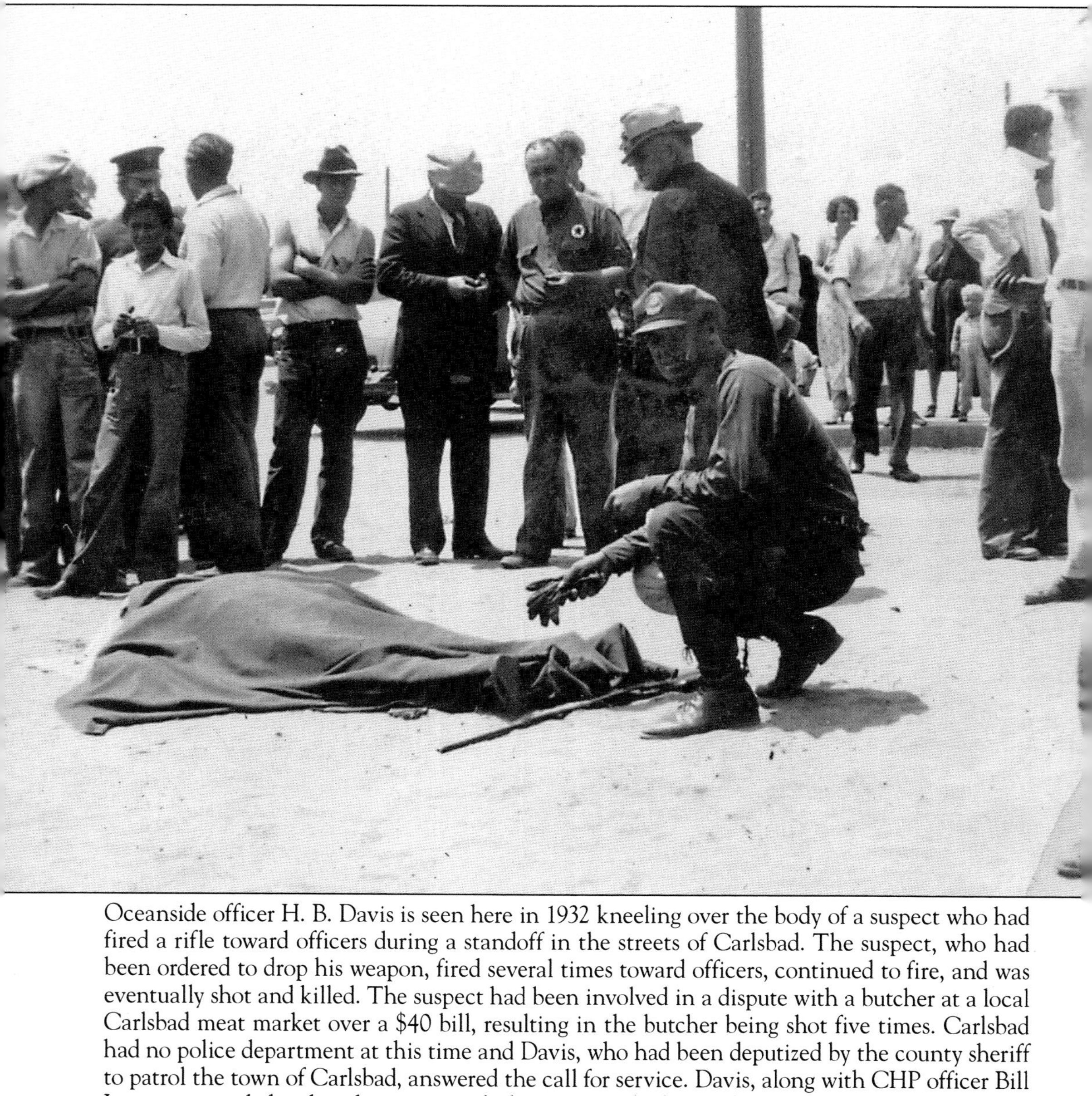

Oceanside officer H. B. Davis is seen here in 1932 kneeling over the body of a suspect who had fired a rifle toward officers during a standoff in the streets of Carlsbad. The suspect, who had been ordered to drop his weapon, fired several times toward officers, continued to fire, and was eventually shot and killed. The suspect had been involved in a dispute with a butcher at a local Carlsbad meat market over a $40 bill, resulting in the butcher being shot five times. Carlsbad had no police department at this time and Davis, who had been deputized by the county sheriff to patrol the town of Carlsbad, answered the call for service. Davis, along with CHP officer Bill Jensen, responded and made contact with the suspect, who began shooting at them. All three men engaged in a gun battle until Bill Jensen ended the nightmare by killing the suspect. (Courtesy Capt. H. B. Davis family.)

Car collisions have plagued American roadways ever since the production of the first Model T in 1908, and Oceanside was no different. Pictured here in 1931, Ofc. H. B. Davis and Chief Charles Goss stand talking in the background of this collision scene, located at Third Street (now Pier View Way) and the railroad crossing, involving a car and a train engine. (Courtesy Capt. H. B. Davis family.)

In 1937, the police department was nine men strong. Pictured, from left to right, outside the old police station located at 305 North Nevada Street, are police chief Warren Paxton; Ofcs. Harold B. Davis, Fred Sickler, Fred Stoner, John Martin, Ernest Taylor, Arthur Pollard, and John Todd; and traffic officer Guy Woodward on the Indian motorcycle. (Courtesy Capt. H. B. Davis family.)

Motorcycle officer Leon Emo looks over a collision scene in 1942, after the driver of this car fell asleep and drove off the roadway into a ditch. Traffic collisions like this were not uncommon and officers still deal with them today, as fatigued drivers are becoming an increasing problem. (Courtesy Capt. H. B. Davis family.)

Sporting his freshly pressed dress uniform, Ofc. Kenneth Hayes, pictured third from the left, smiles on his wedding day on January 1, 1942. Also pictured are his bride, Gladys Hayes, second from the left; her unidentified bridesmaid; and best man, Ofc. H. B. Davis, pictured fourth from the left. (Courtesy Capt. H. B. Davis family.)

Ofc. L. C. Settle, who was hired in 1943, is pictured here in 1944 in downtown Oceanside. Chief of police Warren Paxton observed as Settle intervened and stopped a man from hitting his wife while they stood in the streets of downtown Oceanside. Settle was said to have made short work of the man, thereby saving the woman. Impressed by how he handled himself, Paxton offered Settle a job. Settle worked almost 12 years as an Oceanside officer, rising to the rank of police sergeant. Highly respected by his peers and citizens alike, Settle did not have any problems handling himself on the tough streets of Oceanside. He was fondly referred to as the "Muscle Man of the Goon Squad" by those who worked with him. (Courtesy Capt. H. B. Davis family.)

Motorcycle officer Bill Hoople patrolled aboard his Indian four-cylinder motorcycle after he was hired on May 12, 1938. Unlike motorcycle officers today, motor officer Hoople did not have the benefit of a protective helmet or other protective gear, a police radio, or roadside service should his motorbike break down. (Courtesy Capt. H. B. Davis family.)

On July 20, 1938, all that is left after the traffic collision is the police chalk outline in the middle of Hill Street (now Coast Highway), located between the intersections of Washington Avenue and Minnesota Street. The chalk outline tells the story of a pedestrian who left a local liquor store and, while crossing the street, was struck by a car. Traffic collisions involving pedestrians were common during this time and were often fatal. (Courtesy Capt. H. B. Davis family.)

A call to arms during World War II put Ofc. Kenny Hayes in the military. He is pictured here sometime during the spring of 1945 in his U.S. Army uniform with first sergeant stripes on his sleeve. Standing beside Hayes is Ofc. Harold Davis. (Courtesy Capt. H. B. Davis family.)

During an open house at the Oceanside Fire and Police Department, located at 305 North Nevada Street in 1945, Oceanside fire chief Walter Johnson, police officer H. B. Davis, and Oceanside police chief William Coyle pause to talk and grab a smoke. The departments shared the same building at this time, along with the city hall, city court, city jail, and an office for the CHP. (Courtesy Capt. H. B. Davis family.)

Ofcs. Harold B. Davis and Ernest Henry were hired to the Oceanside Police Department around the same time. Pictured here sporting smart-looking bow ties and standing tall, they are all smiles in the police uniforms that they pieced together from used military uniforms and truck-driver hats. The writing on the back of this photograph reads, "Pals, August 1933, Oceanside, Calif." The following year, in 1934, Charles Goss retired and Ernest Henry became the chief of police. He held that office for two years until he requested to return as a motor officer. Under Henry's leadership in 1935, the first police radio was installed into a patrol car, referred to by officers as a prowl car. (Courtesy Capt. H. B. Davis family.)

This traffic collision in Oceanside, California, was investigated by Ofc. H. B. Davis during the 1940s. It involved a U.S. Navy submarine officer, who was the driver. Officer Davis's notes concerning this photograph read as follows: "No Joke! The driver of this car was an officer on a submarine, but he had his wife with him when he submerged his car. They both came to the station to dry out!" (Courtesy Capt. H. B. Davis family.)

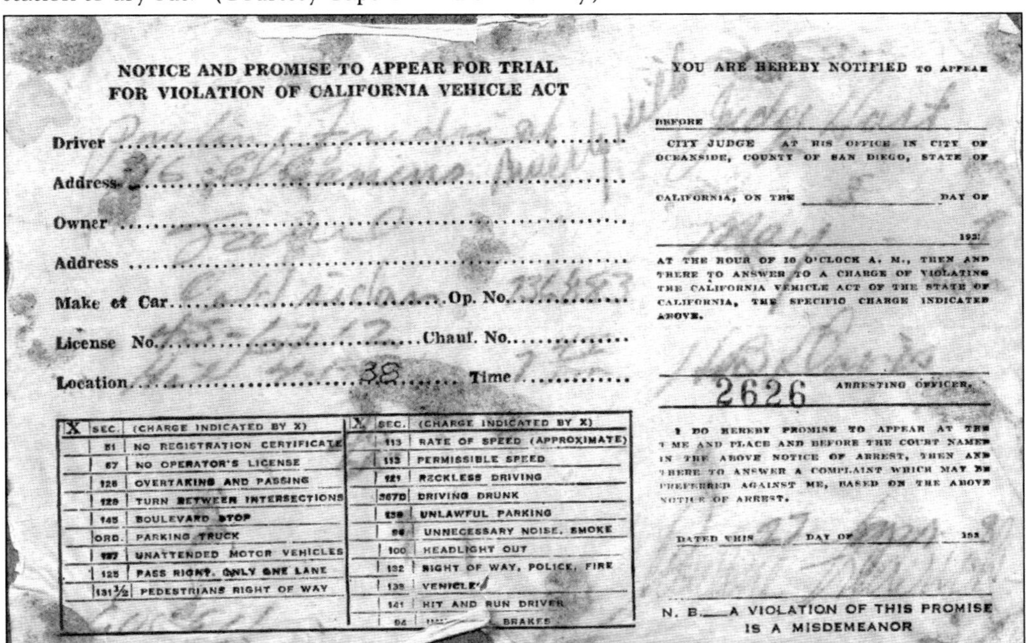

NOTICE AND PROMISE TO APPEAR FOR TRIAL FOR VIOLATION OF CALIFORNIA VEHICLE ACT

Driver ....

Address ....

Owner ....

Address ....

Make of Car .... Op. No. ....

License No. .... Chauf. No. ....

Location .... 38 .... Time ....

X	SEC.	(CHARGE INDICATED BY X)	X	SEC.	(CHARGE INDICATED BY X)
	81	NO REGISTRATION CERTIFICATE		113	RATE OF SPEED (APPROXIMATE)
	67	NO OPERATOR'S LICENSE		113	PERMISSIBLE SPEED
	128	OVERTAKING AND PASSING		121	RECKLESS DRIVING
	129	TURN BETWEEN INTERSECTIONS		367D	DRIVING DRUNK
	145	BOULEVARD STOP		[illegible]	UNLAWFUL PARKING
	ORD.	PARKING TRUCK		[illegible]	UNNECESSARY NOISE, SMOKE
	[illegible]	UNATTENDED MOTOR VEHICLES		100	HEADLIGHT OUT
	125	PASS RIGHT, ONLY ONE LANE		132	RIGHT OF WAY, POLICE, FIRE
	131½	PEDESTRIANS RIGHT OF WAY		139	VEHICLE
				141	HIT AND RUN DRIVER
				94	[illegible] BRAKES

YOU ARE HEREBY NOTIFIED TO APPEAR BEFORE CITY JUDGE AT HIS OFFICE IN CITY OF OCEANSIDE, COUNTY OF SAN DIEGO, STATE OF CALIFORNIA, ON THE .... DAY OF 193

AT THE HOUR OF 10 O'CLOCK A. M., THEN AND THERE TO ANSWER TO A CHARGE OF VIOLATING THE CALIFORNIA VEHICLE ACT OF THE STATE OF CALIFORNIA, THE SPECIFIC CHARGE INDICATED ABOVE.

2626 ARRESTING OFFICER.

I DO HEREBY PROMISE TO APPEAR AT THE TIME AND PLACE AND BEFORE THE COURT NAMED IN THE ABOVE NOTICE OF ARREST, THEN AND THERE TO ANSWER A COMPLAINT WHICH MAY BE PREFERRED AGAINST ME, BASED ON THE ABOVE NOTICE OF ARREST.

DATED THIS .... DAY OF 193

N. B.—A VIOLATION OF THIS PROMISE IS A MISDEMEANOR

Southern California is no stranger to movie stars, and police often came in contact with them. Traffic ticket No. 2626 was issued on May 3, 1938, by Capt. H. B. Davis to silent film star Pauline Fredericks of Beverly Hills, California, for speeding 40 miles per hour in a 25-miles-per-hour zone. Fredericks, whose final film was 1937's "*Thank you, Mr. Moto*," died unexpectedly in September 1938, due to complications from an asthma attack. (Courtesy Capt. H. B. Davis family.)

This 1940 Oceanside police Ford Coup, driven by Capt. Harold Davis and traveling at speeds between 97 and 103 miles per hour, made a quick trip from Oceanside to San Diego, while chasing a Laguna Beach car thief. The front-end damage to the car occurred when the stolen Buick (pictured below), driven by a 16-year-old juvenile delinquent, stopped unexpectedly and the two cars collided. The young suspect was eventually arrested by Captain Davis. (Courtesy Capt. H. B. Davis family.)

During a high-speed chase from Oceanside to San Diego, Capt. H. B. Davis followed close behind this Buick stolen from Laguna Beach. During the chase near Cardiff, California, Captain Davis used his police sidearm to shoot at the Buick, striking it twice in the left rear fender in an attempt to hit the gas tank. The damage to the trunk was caused when the car thief stopped unexpectedly and Captain Davis's police car rear-ended it. Two bullet holes are visible on the left rear side of the stolen car. (Courtesy Capt. H. B. Davis family.)

In 1942, citizens look on as motorcycle officer Guy Woodward lies injured with a broken leg in the intersection of Fifth Street (now Sportfisher Way) and Nevada Street. While chasing one car, Woodward was hit by another one. The ambulance attendant prepares the gurney that took Woodward to the Oceanside hospital. (Courtesy Capt. H. B. Davis family.)

In 1941, Chief Warren Paxton speaks with a citizen at the scene of a traffic collision in Oceanside, while the woman who had been driving was wheeled off on a gurney and taken to the hospital. The driver had made a U-turn at the wrong time and collided with another car. (Courtesy Capt. H. B. Davis family.)

Police officer Jack Leonard is pictured here in 1942, sitting on his Harley Davidson police motorcycle; he was hired by the department sometime the same year. He worked a year and resigned on October 1, 1943. Leonard wanted to trade in his motorcycle officer's wings, seen here, for a set of aviator's wings and pursue a career in aviation with the military. (Courtesy Capt. H. B. Davis family.)

This 1936 photograph, taken near the elementary school, was used to create a postcard that was later sold in local shops to generate funds for the Oceanside Police Department School Safety Crossing Guards Program. The boys seen here all wore a standard-colored sweater, standardized hats, and numbered badges that appointed them as junior police for Oceanside. The men standing behind the young school safety traffic officers are the local businessmen and civic leaders who supported this project. The men pictured here, from left to right, are Chief Warren Paxton, Tom Hurley, Dr. Harold Taylor, Charles Pilgrim, Dale Pogue, William Hart, A. A. Post, Gardener Barnard, Jack Tenney, Ike Glasser, and Ofc. Guy Woodward. (Courtesy Capt. H. B. Davis family.)

This six-point star, badge No. 3, is an original badge worn by a member of the Oceanside Police Department School Safety Crossing Guards during the 1930s. It reads, "Junior Police, Number 3, Traffic Officer, Oceanside." It was one of several issued to the boys who participated in this program to help increase safety in and around their schools. This badge is rare and considered very collectable. (Courtesy Capt. H. B. Davis family.)

On July 24, 1945, Chief William Coyle and Capt. H. B. Davis inventory-seized opium valued at $18,000. The opium was discovered in a car driven by two Chinese nationals who were headed for San Francisco but had been involved in a traffic collision on Highway 101. The drug smugglers were later released to U.S. marshals and U.S. Customs officers after being discharged from the local hospital for injuries sustained in the collision. (Courtesy Capt. H. B. Davis family.)

This vintage postcard illustrates how Oceanside looked to police officers as they patrolled south on Hill Street (now Coast Highway) near Second Street (now Mission Avenue) during the late 1940s. The text on the back explains how Oceanside was famous for its bathing beaches and fishing pier and was a thriving modern city. (Courtesy Matthew J. Lyons.)

The relationship between a field training officer (FTO) and the new police officer trainee is a close one. Some might even say that the FTO "carries" the trainee until he or she can go out on their own. This cartoon, dated July 1, 1941, and drawn by Ofc. Kenny Hayes, demonstrates his light-hearted humor and how it might have seemed to be in a training car with FTO Capt. H. B. Davis. Davis is the driver, and the officer in his lap is Hayes. Davis and Hayes were good friends for many years and like most officers, then and now, learned to expect a little good-natured ribbing every now and then. (Courtesy Capt. H. B. Davis family.)

The Policeman's Ball was a common fund-raising method by police unions to assist officers who were out of work due to injuries sustained on the job. This 1950s ticket admitted one couple to the Oceanside Policeman's Ball held at the American Legion Hall for $1. Entertainment was provided by the Texas Outlaws Radio Orchestra from Beverly Hills, and the backside of the ticket encouraged patrons to meet after the dance at the M&M Bar-B-Q. (Courtesy Capt. H. B. Davis family.)

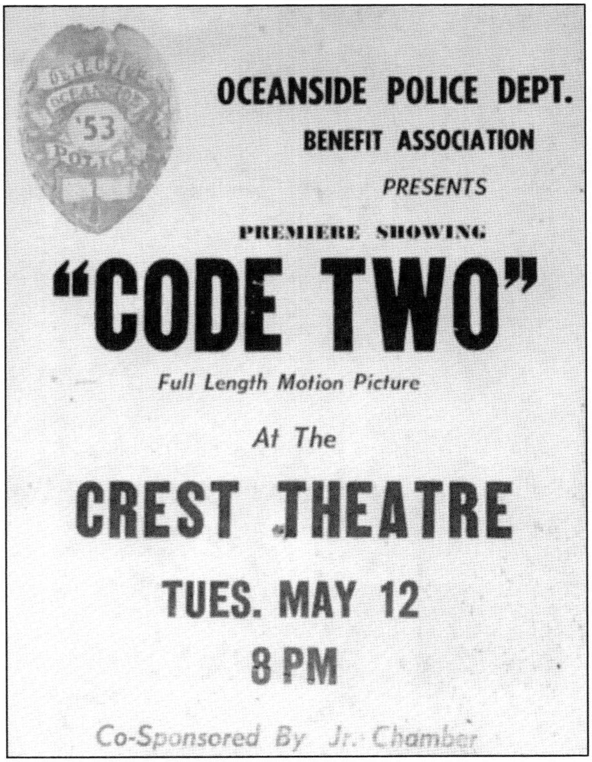

The public's curiosity with the police has always been strong. In 1953, this poster advertised the premiere showing of a "*Dragnet*-style" movie entitled *Code Two*, directed by Fred Wilcox. It featured three young officers attending the police academy and experiencing the trials and tribulations during their first days on the job. The Oceanside Police Department Benefit Association sponsored its showing at the Crest Theatre in Oceanside on May 12, 1953. (Courtesy Capt. H. B. Davis family.)

On September 15, 1952, Edwin W. Patrick was appointed Oceanside's chief of police. Patrick took over the department when crime, locally, was at an all-time high. Although he made progress with the department, revived the police reserve program with 55 members, and increased morale slightly, his career succumbed to internal department problems. He resigned as chief on October 24, 1954. (Courtesy Capt. H. B. Davis family.)

Capt. Harold B. Davis and Ofc. Bill Keenan stand beside their Chevrolet Bel Air police car in 1952, before going to work at 1600 hours. Captain Davis retired in 1955, and Officer Keenan would later test for the San Diego Sheriff's Department and be hired. (Courtesy Capt. H. B. Davis family.)

In 1943, police patrols were beefed up with U.S. Marine Corps Military Policemen (MPs) due to the influx of off-duty Marines from Camp Pendleton. The old city jail was turned over to them for use as a police station from 1943 until 1955, when the MPs moved to their own facility at Cleveland and Michigan. Pictured on February 18, 1955, are some of the last MPs to use the old jail. The MPs patrolled the streets of Oceanside until 1978, when they ceased off-base patrols. (Courtesy Oceanside Police Department Archives.)

In 1947, seated in the chief of police office, located at 305 North Nevada Street, police chief Guy Woodward (seated left) discusses deployment of directed patrols and problem areas with the

Camp Pendleton Military Police watch commander, seated right. (Courtesy Oceanside Police Department Archives.)

The sharing of information between agencies is an important part of controlling crime and keeping a community safe. In downtown Oceanside during the 1940s, MPs from the nearby Camp Pendleton Military Police Department speak briefly with an unidentified Oceanside motor officer on a Harley Davidson. The MPs initially patrolled the city in World War II–era Jeeps, then military police cars. The MPs wore black armbands with white lettering. The Oceanside shoulder patch on the motor officer, adopted sometime during the 1940s, is the only design ever used by Oceanside police. (Courtesy Oceanside Police Department Archives.)

From the 1940s to the late 1970s, the Camp Pendleton Military Police were an important part of the policing duties in Oceanside and often worked in pairs. This photograph, taken in a downtown bar sometime during the 1950s, provided an excellent view into Oceanside's past, showing two MPs checking a Marine's liberty card and sobriety. (Courtesy Oceanside Police Department Archives.)

Pictured here in 1954 near Missouri Street, Patrolman Robert N. Baumgartner poses with his new 1954 Chevy Bel Air police car, complete with two spotlights and a solid red combination light and siren on the roof. He is wearing the tan uniform, changed from the blue one in 1950. Baumgartner was hired on September 14, 1950, and worked in both the Patrol and Detective Divisions. He left to work for the Orange County Sheriff's Department after 1955. (Courtesy Oceanside Police Department Archives.)

Capt. Harold Davis is sitting at his desk as acting chief of police just before his retirement on June 30, 1955, after 25 years of service with the Oceanside Police Department. Captain Davis was acting chief of police six times in 12 years and was the first Oceanside officer to receive a pension. The city council, knowing Davis would be retiring soon, passed Proposition No. 2 that picked up the tab of $10,000 for a pension since Davis had not paid into social security and no pension plan had existed during his tenure. (Courtesy Capt. H. B. Davis family.)

On May 3, 1940, at 3:00 p.m., an unidentified bus driver stands in the street to direct traffic while the Oceanside police investigate a traffic collision on Highway 101 in downtown Oceanside, California. This Model A was traveling southbound and the driver attempted to make a left-hand turn and cross traffic in front of a Sante Fe commercial bus traveling northbound to Los Angeles. The result was a collision that carried the Model A Coupe several hundred feet, made evident by the skid marks. A 1937 Ford Coupe police car is seen in the distance, parked just behind the bus. (Courtesy Capt. H. B. Davis family.)

Det. Lt. William D. Sprouse Sr. is pictured here pointing at some recovered stolen property and other contraband in the parking lot just outside the police station at 305 North Nevada Street. It was common at that time for detectives to wear full suits and matching fedora hats, regardless of the weather and heat. (Courtesy Oceanside Police Department Archives.)

In an unprecedented event, Captain Davis scratches his head while his wife, Alma, looks over the pink slip of a new car being presented to them. The citizens of Oceanside presented both of them with a brand new 1955 Chevrolet Bel Air sport coupe model sedan that was paid in full in appreciation for Captain Davis's many years of service to the community as a policeman. (Courtesy Capt. H. B. Davis family.)

Alma Davis, the devoted wife of Capt. Harold Davis, is pictured here waving to parade watchers as Captain Davis drives up Hill Street during a Fourth of July parade in the Chevrolet they received from the citizens of Oceanside in 1955. It is often said the toughest job in police work is the job of a policeman's wife, because they do so much behind the scenes. If that is true, then Alma Davis deserved this car more than Harold. (Courtesy Capt. H. B. Davis family.)

Ofc. L. C. Settle is pictured here "hamming it up" for the camera during the 1958 Days of San Luis Rey Fiesta and Rodeo, in which he often dressed up in various forms of period clothing. Although he never would be elected sheriff of San Diego County, Officer Settle was known to many as the sheriff of San Luis Rey. (Courtesy L. C. Settle family.)

L. C. Settle was born in Strong City, Oklahoma, and moved to California when he was 16 years old. He worked 12 years with the Oceanside Police Department, until he started up a security company under his own name. A well-respected and likable member of the community, L. C. Settle ran for San Diego County sheriff in 1958 and created this handbill. Although L. C. Settle was not elected sheriff, he made lifelong friends and continued his work in private industry. (Courtesy L. C. Settle family.)

Ofc. L. C. Settle, an experienced cowboy, was well known throughout California for his riding skills and showmanship. Settle brought smiles to many an audience when he participated in hundreds of community events, rodeos, and parades, including the Rose Parade in Pasadena. He is pictured here showing off some of his skills and confidence on horseback, making it appear easy. A true gentleman from simpler but tougher times, Officer Settle passed away on March 31, 2005, leaving a void in the Oceanside landscape. He will be greatly missed, but his memory as a firm but fair, straight-talking policeman will remain etched in Oceanside police history. (Courtesy L. C. Settle family.)

In 1945, Leon Emo, in his U.S. Army Air Corps uniform, stands in front of the home of Ofc. H. B. Davis, who joins him in this photograph. Emo, a former Oceanside police officer, stopped to visit his friend on his way from Barstow, California, to New Mexico, for additional training in aviation. (Courtesy Capt. H. B. Davis family.)

In 1943, Ofc. Lowell Settle investigates this tractor-trailer collision at the intersection of Highway 101 and Vista Way in Oceanside, California. The load of lumber in the back of this truck shifted as it was rounding the corner and caused the truck to tip over. No one was injured in the accident, but traffic was blocked for several hours until equipment could be brought in to remove the load and upright the truck. (Courtesy Capt. H. B. Davis family.)

This 1941 Plymouth police squad car, parked in front of the old Oceanside jail at Oceanside's Heritage Park, was restored by Ofcs. Dan Shapiro, Richard Derouen, and Dale Wood in 1983. The car is used for public relations and other civic events like parades and ceremonies to foster a sense of history and appreciation for the officers who went before them. (Courtesy Capt. H. B. Davis family.)

Ofc. Jack Hunton stands beside his motorcycle and looks over a traffic collision at Hill Street (now Coast Highway) and Michigan Street near the Oceanside Ford garage. The driver of the flatbed truck in the distance fell asleep and sideswiped the two cars parked on the side of the road. No one was injured in this collision. (Courtesy Capt. H. B. Davis family.)

On January 1, 1944, Oceanside policemen and Camp Pendleton MPs investigate a multiple-traffic collision at the Sante Fe Railroad underpass on Highway 101, located just north of Oceanside. A caravan of military trucks was traveling southbound, and a civilian truck towing another was traveling northbound when a coupe attempted to pass the caravan of military trucks. The coupe went between the lanes of travel, striking the tow truck and causing all the vehicles to collide into each other. (Courtesy Capt. H. B. Davis family.)

In the 1930s, Mary Todd was hired as a police matron. She is considered Oceanside Police Department's first woman officer. Mary Todd worked a total of 30 years with the police department in different capacities ranging from chief's secretary, to answering telephones, to searching female prisoners, etc. When Todd received a call for service, she would flip on a switch that turned on a red light attached to a 40-foot pole on top of the police station. Patrolling officers would see the light and return to the station to get the information for the call for service. On May 1, 1962, Mary Todd retired. (Courtesy Capt. H. B. Davis family.)

Chief of police William Wingard, pictured here in a 1962 photograph, served as chief from 1955 to 1962. He is credited with increasing the size of the police department to 38 officers, including the position of chief. Chief Wingard improved professionalism by requiring all new officers to attend a formal police academy, as required by the newly created Police Officers Standards and Training (POST) commission at the state level. He implemented a standard workweek similar to other professions; officers no longer had to work more than a 40-hour week without overtime. (Courtesy Capt. H. B. Davis family.)

The Oceanside Police Benefit Association (OPBA), at the time of this 1953 photograph, consisted of all police members, including captain's rank and below. This OPBA-sponsored picnic and cookout was held at Buddy Todd Park, named for the son of Mary Todd, who was killed in World War II and was an accomplished Oceanside surfer. Everyone from the department who did not have to stay on duty attended. Pictured, from left to right, are (first row) motor officers J. P. Stafford and H. Moore; (second row) motor officer H. C. Russell, motor sergeant C. J. O'Haver, Ofc. Bert Winford, Chief E. Patrick (wearing cowboy hat), Ofc. L. W. Howell, Ofc. J. Anderson, Det. J. L. Demoss, Ofc. A. J. Doucet, desk officer P. Ricotta, Ofc. W. R. Barrett, detective sergeant R. Keagy, Det. W. D. Sprouse, L. Gurley, Capt. H. B. Davis (wearing cooking apron), and Sgt. A. H. Dreyer; (third row) Sgt. D. G. Eastman, Det. R. N. Baumgartner, motor officer H. R. Parker, and Det. H. Teakell. (Courtesy Capt. H. B. Davis family.)

Drawn by Jack Wilkerson in the 1930s, this undated cartoon was given to Capt. Harold Davis. It appears to be making fun of an Oceanside traffic officer who is having a bad day and does not want to hear any excuses from the driver he is giving a speeding ticket to. It reads, "My mother-in-law moved in last night, my kid kept me awake, my wife burned my toast, and my coffee was cold. Now I say you were going seventy! What's your story?" (Courtesy Capt. H. B. Davis family.)

This photograph was taken during Christmas 1958 at the old police station at 305 North Nevada Street. Standing in front of a Christmas tree and holiday cards that hung on the wall, from left to right, are Dogcatcher Flowers, Ofc. Lou Howell, and Ofc. Ed McKissick. (Courtesy Oceanside Police Department Archives.)

The Oceanside Police Department (OPD) grew under the leadership of police chief William Wingard. Pictured here in 1962, from left to right, are (first row) Ray Wilkerson, Ernest Michael, Ollie MacDonald (first woman detective), Pauline Lail (early woman officer), police chief William Wingard, Mary Todd (first woman officer), Capt. Ward Ratcliff (10th police chief), Janis Robertson, Helen Barclay, Joseph Stafford, Gary Wade, and John Key (partial image); (second row) Terry Stephens, Floyd Flowers, Gerry Breneman, Ed McKissick, Don Brown, Wiley Tucker, Armand

Doucet, Allen Dryer, William Sprouse, Paul Ricotta, John Quintro, Henry Himmelspach, and John Story (not seen); (third row) Jack Ewers (partial image), Gene Williams, Don Sammons, Jack Sanders, Rex Bennett, Bill Weatherby, C. A. Hughes (first African American officer), Richard Green, E. Erickson, Richard Bingham, H. Russell, Radke, Robert Underhill, Larry Jensen, and Roy Smith (partial image). (Courtesy Capt. H. B. Davis family.)

VOTE "YES"

CITY OF OCEANSIDE, CALIF.

PROPOSITION NO. 2

The economic soundness of the retirement principal as predicated on an employee contributory basis provides closer relationship between local governmental employees and the taxpayer. This is as it should be, for the intimate governmental services performed by City Employees, should afford the closest tie government has with the citizens who make up Oceanside.

Retirement Plan for Municipal Employees

The people of California voted State employees under this Retirement Plan. Do not Municipal workers deserve the same consideration?

Remember to Vote 'YES'

April 13th

Proposition No. 2

This handbill pamphlet, dated April 13, 1955, encouraged Oceanside citizens to vote yes on the City of Oceanside Proposition No. 2, approving the creation of a retirement plan for municipal employees of the city, namely police officers. The proposition passed, and the city approved a one-time lump sum of over $10,000 into the state retirement plan; thereby allowing Capt. H. B. Davis, due to retire shortly after this, the benefit of a pension for his 25 years of honorable service. Future officers could now receive a pension as well, after service as a police officer for 25 or more years. Prior to this, Oceanside police officers received nothing for their years of dedicated service. (Courtesy Capt. H. B. Davis family.)

Three

Men and Women of the OPD

1960s, 1970s, and 1980s

Wearing his game face in 1968, Chief Ratcliff, who was at the helm of the police department through some of Oceanside's toughest years (1962–1975), stands just outside his office at the police station at 1617 Mission Avenue. During his tenure, Ratcliff dealt with racial and social unrest problems that plagued the nation at this time. Additionally, nearby Camp Pendleton, combined with an antiwar movement, created another concern for the strong leader, who was still able to make improvements by increasing officer numbers to 92; adding three police dogs; improving equipment, cars, and facilities; and no longer requiring officers to buy their own uniforms. (Courtesy Oceanside Police Department Archives.)

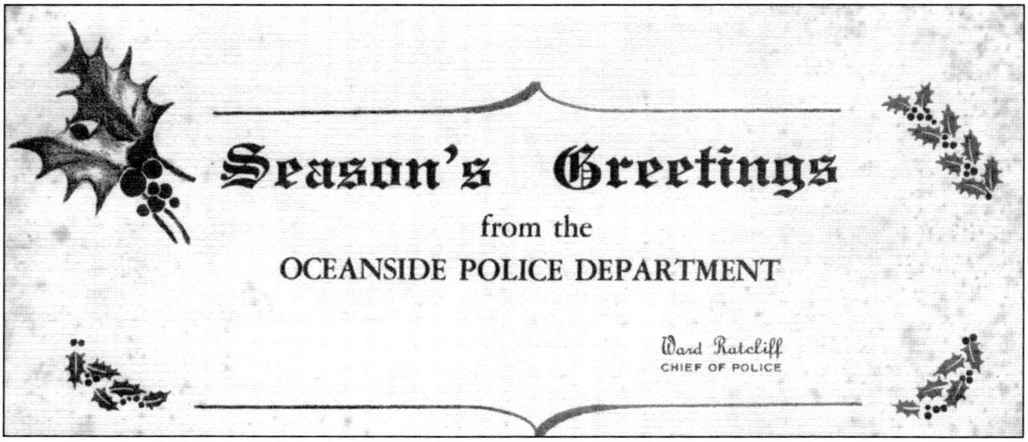

Due to the nature of the job, most police officers work holidays like Christmas and Thanksgiving, but that doesn't mean they don't still have the holiday spirit. Pictured here is a simple Christmas card, *c.* 1960s, sent out from the police department during the Chief Ward Ratcliff administration to community members and friends. (Courtesy L. C. Settle family.)

The job of a police detective is a tedious and time-consuming one that requires an analytical mind, patience, attention to detail, and a desire to follow leads to their ends. Unlike their uniformed counterparts, who are finished with a report at the end of their shift, the detective must stay on top of a case until it is completed or until all leads have been exhausted. Most detectives will have spent many years on the streets as a uniformed police officer, honing their interviewing and investigative skills, before being selected for a transfer into the Detective Division. Pictured here during the 1980s are Dets. Bob Pratt and Bill Donnelly, reviewing leads that might solve their cases. (Courtesy Oceanside Police Department Archives.)

Before the police department created a field evidence technician position, police officers and detectives had to locate, identify, and collect their own evidence at crime scenes. This 1970s photograph shows Det. Bob George dusting for latent fingerprints at a crime scene. (Courtesy Oceanside Police Department Archives.)

OCEANSIDE POLICE FACILITY

DEDICATED MARCH 1968

In 1968, the Oceanside Police Department moved from 305 North Nevada Street to a new police facility at 1617 Mission Avenue. Chief Ward Ratcliff hosted a ceremony dedicating the new building. Created the same year, this program booklet was published by the city to help document this important event in Oceanside police history and highlight some of the new benefits. (Courtesy Oceanside Police Department Archives.)

Pictured here in 1975, Ofc. Dick Frye and his K-9 partner, King, get ready to leave the parking lot of the police station located at 1617 Mission Avenue. The use of police dogs had just recently been adopted by the police department. This old, white AMC Matador police car didn't have much in the way of special equipment and allowed the dog access to the front seat as well. (Courtesy Oceanside Police Department Archives.)

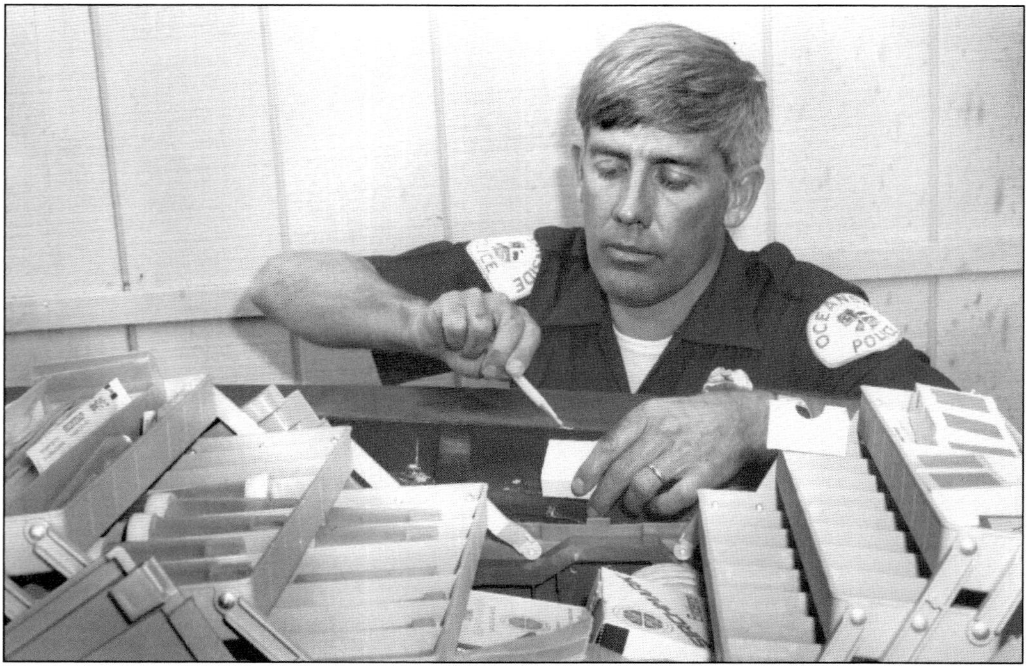

The collection of evidence is a very important part of a police officer's duties. During the 1980s, Ofc. Ron Jenkins carefully places a small fiber into a sterile container for future comparison and analysis. All evidence located at a crime scene is handled with care, ensuring that evidence is properly preserved and documented. (Courtesy Oceanside Police Department Archives.)

According to officers, traffic stops are not routine, especially when it is discovered that the car the officer just stopped was reported stolen or used in a violent crime. This 1995 photograph demonstrates how Ofc. Ernie Thibedeau, who previously worked for the LAPD, would respond to a potential threat from the car he has just stopped. (Courtesy Oceanside Police Department Archives.)

Crowd control is among the many dangerous tasks that police officers undertake. Officers must be able to keep the peace in large crowds, remain calm among angry protesters, and work as a team. This 1983 photograph shows OPD officers with San Diego County deputies in a tactical formation outside the main gate of the Camp Pendleton Marine Corps Base. They are maintaining order as demonstrators hold up signs in protest of the government. (Courtesy Oceanside Police Department Archives.)

An element of many crimes involves some form of emotional reaction to the victim. In this 1985 case, police officers are investigating the vandalism of a trailer that appears to also be a message to the victim. Police officers must look beyond the initial incident to determine if other crimes have been committed and the underlying motives for that crime. (Courtesy Oceanside Police Department Archives.)

This photograph, taken during a night shift in the 1980s, shows senior officer Kevin Kaiser sending an announcement over his police car public address system, with the Dodge Diplomat tactically positioned, while his police dog Tommy awaits command to attack. In 1988, Officer Kaiser and Tommy took first-place honors in the veteran dog division at a competition held at Camp Pendleton, featuring 25 civilian and military police dogs from around the state. Kaiser was a former U.S. Marine police-dog handler. (Courtesy Oceanside Police Department Archives.)

During the early 1980s, Oceanside still had a lot of open land that had yet to be developed, and there was a need for enforcement of those areas. To aid officers in their enforcement duties and to allow easy mobility, a more practical vehicle was proposed. Here an officer drives an off-road emergency vehicle in one of the more remote areas of Oceanside. (Courtesy Oceanside Police Department Archives.)

Oceanside's beaches are considered some of the best in the United States—three-and-a-half miles of gorgeous white sand and breathtaking sunsets. In this undated photograph, Oceanside officers assigned to the beach complete field interview cards while speaking to beach patrons. (Courtesy Oceanside Police Department Archives.)

The Oceanside PD has used motorcycles since the 1930s when Ofc. Warren Paxton patrolled the city. The department stopped motorcycle use in the late 1960s but started again in 1978. Motorcycles allow officers to get to the scene of a traffic collision or other incidents quickly, putting law enforcement on target when they are needed most—at the onset of a problem. This image from the late 1980s depicts motor officers Ron Shedd (foreground) and Gene Fernandez. Oceanside motor officers from bygone years did not wear helmets, but the patches on their sleeves haven't changed much in 50 years. Tradition is upheld in police work and ties these officers to the pioneers of their profession. (Courtesy Oceanside Police Department Archives.)

Area of Impact, or AOI, is what police officers in California call the point where one car collides with another car or object. This 1970s image depicts an unidentified Oceanside traffic officer pointing to where skid marks, left on a road by car tires, began before the car eventually left the roadway. Officers must use mathematic formulas to help them determine speed and direction of cars during their investigations. Documentation of this type of physical evidence helps determine factors that cause the collision. (Courtesy Oceanside Police Department Archives.)

Most people may not want to see the inside of a police car, especially the back seat. However, some might be interested in seeing the front area where a police officer works. This 1984 photograph of Oceanside police officer Dan Ahrens using the radio provides a great view to the various electronic and radio equipment inside this Dodge Diplomat. The shotgun is also mounted to the interior for quick access. (Courtesy Oceanside Police Department Archives.)

The need for administrative manpower, without the cost of sworn officers, generated the idea of non-sworn public service officers (PSOs). Newly hired PSOs are seen here in the 1980s as they train on the computer at the front desk. The PSO title would eventually change to community service officer (CSO) and the job opportunities for CSOs would increase. Today's CSOs work the front desk, cold-case reports, informational services, and as field evidence technicians and investigative assistants. (Courtesy Oceanside Police Department Archives.)

This 1986 photograph shows community service officer Linda Wood and another CSO looking on, as Ofc. Dale Wood receives a plaque from the CSO class that he instructed for four weeks. Wood developed the Oceanside PD CSO Academy and instructed it as well. (Courtesy Oceanside Police Department Archives.)

Pedestrian stops are a prime method for gaining criminal intelligence, but they can be dangerous if not handled properly. This 1990s photograph shows Ofc. Jim Wall standing a safe distance from the subject, who is sitting on a curb in a position of disadvantage. (Courtesy Oceanside Police Department Archives.)

Senior officer Kelan Poorman loads his Mosberg 870 police shotgun during a critical incident in 1983. He is standing behind his Ford black-and-white for cover and concealment. A police officer must be able to react quickly at the first indication of danger and lock down a situation, whenever possible, until additional officers and resources can be deployed. (Courtesy Oceanside Police Department Archives.)

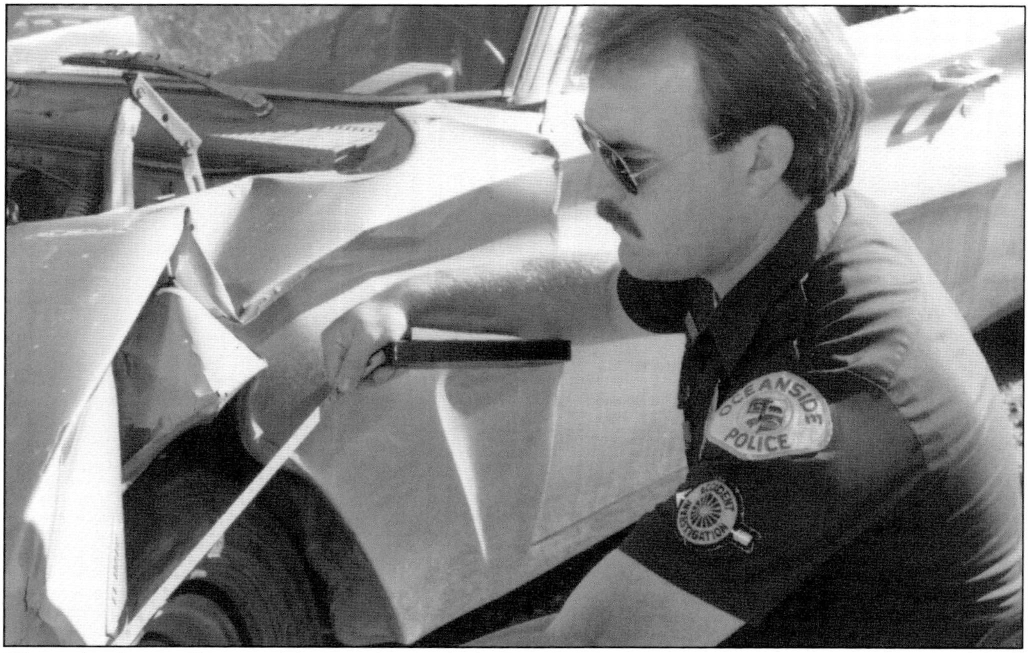

The job of a traffic accident investigator has continued to be a vital part of the Oceanside Police Department ever since Guy Woodward and Harold Davis were on patrol in the 1930s. Accident investigator reconstructionists take measurements to determine the speed at the time of collisions. Pictured here during the 1980s, an unidentified traffic officer takes measurements while investigating the physical evidence of this car involved in a traffic collision. (Courtesy Oceanside Police Department Archives.)

Chief Laurence Marshal is pictured here in the mid-1980s at the police station, located at 1617 Mission Avenue. Chief Marshal was in charge of OPD, one California's busiest city police departments, from 1981 to 1987. Chief Marshal, the former under-sheriff of Santa Barbara County, was more than able to address any problems that he might encounter. (Courtesy Oceanside Police Department Archives.)

In this 1970s image, two unidentified detectives role-play as suspects in a high-risk traffic stop. They are using their 1968 Dodge Polara detective car as two unidentified uniformed police officers, also role-playing, give them commands to put their hands in the air. Training for a police officer is instrumental for a uniformed response to a crisis or critical incident. Many times, what officers learn in training is what they will do during a real incident. (Courtesy Oceanside Police Department Archives.)

Many African Americans have made considerable contributions to their communities. The city of Oceanside was fortunate to have one such man who decided to stand on the "Thin Blue Line" and become a police officer. This police identification photograph of Ofc. Curtis Hughes was taken during the mid-1970s, early in his career. Hughes was the first African American officer to work for the Oceanside Police Department. He was hired on February 15, 1961, and rose to the rank of sergeant, marking yet another milestone as the first African American to attain that rank in the OPD. His contributions were many, and he will not be forgotten. (Courtesy Oceanside Police Department Archives.)

Sunday, January 12, 1975 The Blade-Tribune—19

OCEANSIDE policemen Frank Brock (left) and Steve Scarano deliver rabbits to students.

Community policing is necessary in any city, and making a difference in the schools with young people is equally important. This Sunday, January 12, 1975 edition of the *Blade-Tribune* newspaper clipping was written and photographed by Wyman Dunlap and is entitled "Oceanside Police Replace Rabbit at Garrison School." The story features Ofcs. Frank Brock and Steve Scarrano delivering rabbits to the students of the aforementioned school after vandals had entered the school grounds and stolen them. (Courtesy *North County Times*.)

Pictured here in a tan uniform during the late 1970s is Ofc. Edie Cindrich (now Edie Faylor), who was hired on April 7, 1974, to work as a patrol officer. Unlike the pioneering women who had preceded her, Cindrich would be the first female officer to work a beat and patrol alone in a car. Quoted in the Sunday, April 7, 1974, edition of the *Blade-Tribune,* Cindrich said that she planned "to be very polite" if ever sent to a bar to handle three drunken, burly customers. Given the volume of violent calls for service handled by police officers at that time, Cindrich certainly handled those types of incidents. (Courtesy Oceanside Police Department Archives.)

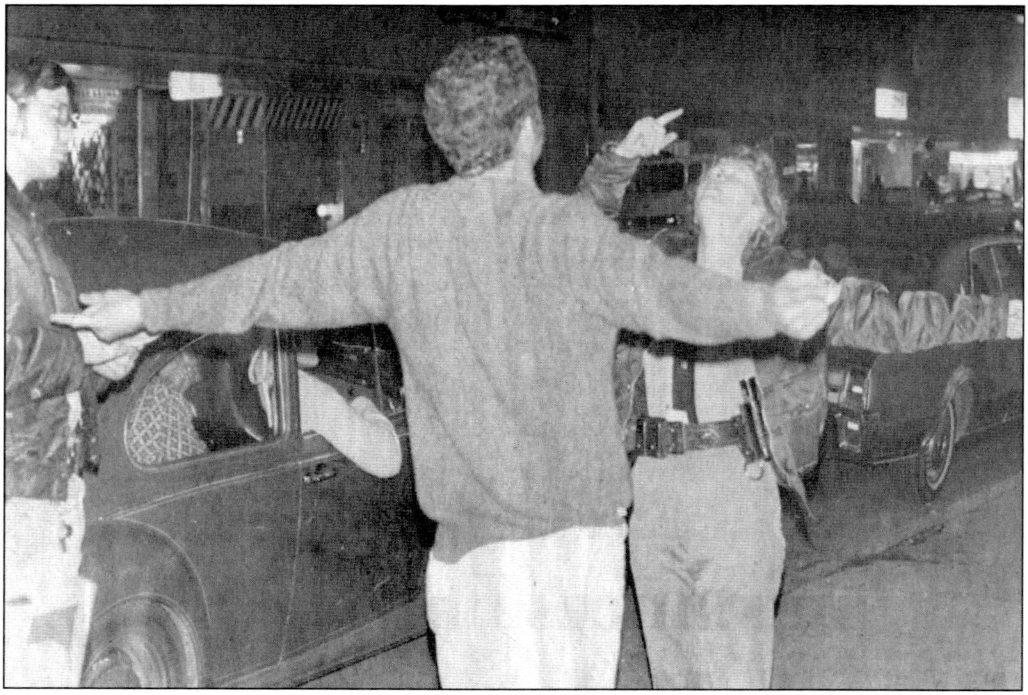

This undated (possibly late 1970s) newspaper clipping from the *Blade-Tribune* of an article written and photographed by Wyman Dunlap is entitled "Oceanside Police Patrols after 'Drinking Drivers.'" Officers are depicted conducting a field sobriety test of the driver. The caption reads, "Field Sobriety Test is demonstrated by OPD officer Edie Cindrich while Ralph Korbacher takes notes." (Courtesy *North County Times*.)

At the back of the Oceanside Police Department in 1989, a group of dispatchers show their Christmas spirit as they take a well-deserved break to pose for this photograph. (Courtesy Oceanside Police Department Archives.)

Shot in the line of duty with only four years on the job, Ofc. Chuck Potter stood on the symbolic "Thin Blue Line." Potter, pictured here in the 1970s, was hired on August 7, 1972. On January 18, 1976, at 10:00 a.m., Potter responded to cover Ofc. Mike Gray on a call involving a man and woman fighting in the streets at Sixth and Tremont. Upon arrival, the police found that the couple had separated, and Potter contacted the male subject who, unknown to Potter, was a prison escapee. The subject asked to reach for his identification and instead pulled out a handgun, pointing it at Officer Potter's head. Potter blocked the gun by pulling the subject's arm down and away, just as the subject pulled the trigger. The bullet entered Potter's leg and, as he fell, Officer Gray pulled his service weapon and returned fire as his pistol cleared its holster. Three bullets struck the subject, and the unprovoked attack ended along with his life. Officer Potter recovered from his injuries, returning to full duty, and later worked as a detective with the police department. (Courtesy Oceanside Police Department Archives.)

Breaking the glass ceiling is tough, but it was even tougher in the 1950s when Det. Ollie MacDonald was hired as a police officer. Hired on October 23, 1956, MacDonald proved herself a competent and professional officer in a time when few women worked in the law enforcement profession. Seen here in this late-1970s photograph, Ollie MacDonald paved the way for women officers who would follow her and is credited as being the first female officer to become a detective with the Oceanside Police Department. (Courtesy Oceanside Police Department Archives.)

In this early 1980s photograph, from left to right, are chief of police Rolf A. Henze, evidence custodian Bill McCarthy, and jailer Bill Cox in the chief's office at the Oceanside PD at 1617 Mission Avenue. Jailers and evidence custodians were non-sworn personnel, similar to the community service officer position of today. (Courtesy Shirl Tyner collection.)

Much like an air traffic controller, who must know plane locations in air space, a police dispatcher must know the whereabouts and status of each patrol car while still managing calls into the communications center. Oceanside police dispatchers provide communications for not only the police but the fire department and other emergency services. In 1989, Marie Legg, wearing a white uniform shirt with Oceanside police patches on her shoulders, was a communications professional. She is sitting at the primary radio dispatching terminal wearing a radio/telephone headset. Police officers depend on dispatchers for information that will help result in safety and efficiency. Dispatchers learn to operate advanced radio equipment and to speak succinctly without emotional overtones under the pressure of 911 emergency calls. (Courtesy Oceanside Police Department Archives.)

Considered by many as one of the most upbeat and positive people one could ever meet, Ofc. Oscar Mayo was a major asset to the Oceanside PD. Hired on June 21, 1971, he was the first Latino officer in the department. Officer Mayo would later work as a detective. (Courtesy Oceanside Police Department Archives.)

In this 1986 photograph, Oceanside detective Oscar Mayo kisses fellow detective Bob Pratt. This is a perfect example of not taking one's self too seriously in the business of police work. Pratt, who was hired on April 15, 1968, is a good sport while Mayo horses around to the amusement of the Detective Division. Police clerk/matron Hertie Wilson, who was hired on August 1, 1967, laughs at the antics. She is credited as the first black female woman hired by the OPD. (Courtesy Oceanside Police Department Archives.)

The city of Oceanside is a racially diverse community, including many with Pacific Islander, or more specifically, Samoan heritage. This police identification photograph from the late 1970s is of Ofc. Larry Faumuina, considered the first Pacific Islander officer to work for the Oceanside Police Department. He was hired on September 1, 1972, and retired after 20 years of honorable service. Officer Faumuina later worked for the San Diego County District Attorney's office as an investigator. On October 5, 2004, he died at age 55 of natural causes. (Courtesy Oceanside Police Department Archives.)

Thursday, March 7, 1974

BEACH PLUNGE — A 22-year-old Oceanside man received minor injuries about 1:15 p.m. Wednesday when his 1963 Chevrolet plunged into the ocean at the foot of Wisconsin Street, police said. Richard Gary Millerbus, 601 Capistrano, was in sastisfactory condition at Tri-City Hospital today. Police said there was no evidence that the driver took any action to stop before hitting the water. (Bill Carman Photo)

Dated Thursday, March 7, 1974, this newspaper clipping from the *Blade-Tribune*, photographed by Bill Carman, is captioned "Beach Plunge." Oceanside police officer Bob Pratt assists a driver who drove his "1963 Chevrolet" into the ocean "at the foot of Wisconsin Street." (Courtesy *North County Times*.)

Southern California has the most actors per capita than any other state, so Oceanside sees its share of Hollywood stars. British actor Christopher Lee, pictured here sometime during the 1970s, is seated in the officer's lounge to the far left. Lee was visiting a friend, reserve police officer Sandy Zuckerman (standing behind him), and observed her for a ride-around on patrol. He also shared a cup of coffee with officers. Lee has appeared in more than 100 films, including *The Man with the Golden Gun* (1974), the *Lord of the Rings* trilogy, *Star Wars Episode II: Attack of the Clones* (2002), *Charlie and the Chocolate Factory* (2005), and *Harry Potter and the Goblet of Fire* (2005). Pictured here, from left to right, are Christopher Lee, Lt. Bob Smith, Det. Bob Pratt, Sandy Zuckerman, unidentified, and patrol sergeant C. C. Sanders. (Courtesy Oceanside Police Department Archives.)

This late-1980s photograph features an unidentified Oceanside traffic officer. Traffic duties included speed enforcement with the use of a handheld radar gun. In most surveys, the No. 1 concern or complaint for citizens is traffic enforcement and speed. Oceanside, like most major police departments, maintains a separate section within the police department dedicated to such concerns. Officers, going in and out of traffic, identify problems and try to solve and decrease violations. Each time an officer stops a car on the roadway, that officer's life and personal safety is put in danger by the "5,000-pound missiles"—motor vehicles—speeding by. (Courtesy Oceanside Police Department Archives.)

Four

THE OCEANSIDE POLICE DEPARTMENT 1990S–2005

This mural, matching the images on the badges that officers wear, is located on the front of the current Oceanside PD headquarters, which opened in 1997 at 3855 Mission Avenue. The small and outdated former police station at 1617 Mission Avenue became obsolete for the growing city. With two buildings and a large, secure parking area, the new location on the corner of El Camino Real was a more centralized location and allowed ready access to Highway 76 and quicker response to calls for service. (Courtesy Matthew J. Lyons.)

It can be said that the front desk of any police station is the spearhead of information services that connects the community with the department. Pictured here in this early 1990s photograph is an unidentified community service officer assisting a citizen at the front desk of the police station, located at 1617 Mission Avenue. (Courtesy Oceanside Police Department Archives.)

Ofc. Richard Anderson is pictured here with his police K-9, Boss, in the mid-1980s. In 1988, Officer Anderson and Boss took second place honors in the searching competition held at Camp Pendleton; it featured 25 civilian and military police dogs from around the state of California. Officer Anderson was hired on December 8, 1981, and had several years in law enforcement experience before coming to OPD. (Courtesy Oceanside Police Department Archives.)

Pictured here in the 1980s are two of Oceanside most identifiable symbols—the pier, which is able to withstand rough storms, and Dennis Thornton, a seasoned police officer, able to withstand the storms of life. On a sunny March morning in 1998, Officer Thornton responded to a report of a hit-and-run collision in which one party had not exchanged information and fled the scene. The second party pursued the first driver to his home. The fleeing suspect was in the house and refused to come out. While Officer Thornton began to investigate the collision, the suspect abruptly came out with a .38-caliber handgun and shot Officer Thornton once in the face. Severely wounded, Officer Thornton, required numerous surgeries to repair the severed nerves in one of his ears. It caused permanent hearing loss. Thornton returned to work in November, but the hearing loss proved to be a safety risk, forcing him into early retirement. Years later, other medical conditions directly related to this unprovoked attack would begin to show themselves as Officer Thornton grew older. Officer Thornton's attacker was tried and convicted of attempted murder, but the case was later overturned. The suspect was retried and a second jury found the suspect guilty of attempted murder. Officer Thornton continues to work as an investigator for a private law firm in San Diego, keeping a good attitude about his profession and remaining proud. Thornton recently made a light-hearted comment saying, "Knowing what I know today about what was going to happen to me on March 11, 1998, I would still become a police officer. I just would have called in sick on that day!" (Courtesy Thornton personal collection.)

This current Oceanside PD badge was adopted in 1997, similar to the LAPD badge but with Oceanside symbols. The border design is based on the *fasces*, or ancient Roman symbols of authority. The top ribbon designates the rank of the officer. The center has a replica of the Mission San Luis Rey, a key symbol unique to Oceanside and California's historic beginnings. Behind the mission are rays from a setting sun to represent a West Coast location. The city seal is divided into quarters—a mission to reflect California's Spanish history, a bear symbolizing the state, a fish to denote Oceanside's fishing industry and connection to the ocean, and a cornucopia for the bounty that city has to offer. The middle ribbon designates the city and department. The third ribbon designates the badge number or rank by stars. (Courtesy Oceanside Police Department Archives.)

When the San Luis Rey River (normally a dry bed) overflowed its banks in January 1993, several Oceanside police officers and Oceanside Harbor District police officers assisted the Oceanside Fire Department in a swift-water rescue near 4841 North River Road. During most of the year, homeless and transient persons reside in the riverbed in makeshift huts and tents. (Courtesy Oceanside Police Department Archives.)

Lt. Sheila Potkonjak, pictured here in 1999, was hired by the OPD on November 11, 1979, as a police officer with the same assigned duties as her male counterparts. She worked in the Patrol Division NETWORK, a community-based gang enforcement program, and Detective Division, from which she eventually retired in 2003. In 1999, she was promoted to sergeant and is considered the Oceanside Police Department's first woman officer to attain that rank. While working in that position, Sgt. Potkonjak was responsible for the department's recruiting, training academy, reserve officer program, citizen academy, and public relations. In 2001, Potkonjak was promoted to lieutenant, the first female to attain that rank. (Courtesy Oceanside Police Department Archives.)

On June 13, 2003, at about 5:00 p.m., Ofc. Tony W. Zeppetella conducted a traffic stop of a car in the parking lot of the Navy Federal Credit Union, which was busy with payday customers. The credit union, located on the corner of College Boulevard and Avenida De La Plata in Oceanside, must have seemed like the last place for anything to happen. This traffic stop was like so many others, except it quickly became the worst of all situations. Unknown to Officer Zeppetella, the driver was a gang member in possession of illegal narcotics and a handgun. During the stop, the suspect shot and mortally wounded Officer Zeppetella, who fell while exchanging gunfire with the suspect, striking him once. Officer Zeppetella lost his life but won the hearts of his peers and the community for his steadfast response to a no-win situation. The killer was found guilty of murder and sentenced to death in 2006. Officer Zeppetella left behind a wife and young child, parents, and countless friends and admirers. This funeral program commemorates his life. (Courtesy Oceanside Police Department Archives.)

The Oceanside Fallen Officers Memorial at the entrance of the current police department was created in 2003 and is visible to both the officers who are leaving the station to patrol the city and the public. Inscribed on this black marble stone monument are three names: City Marshals Charlie C. Wilson, EOW: July 4, 1889; John Mugan, EOW: September 24, 1916; and Ofc. Tony Zeppetella, EOW: June 13, 2003. Each of these officers died in the line of duty by three different murderers across more than a century. But each died doing the same task—making the community a safer place for us all. (Photograph by Matthew J. Lyons.)

This 2005 photograph depicts an Oceanside police Ford Crown Victoria parked next to the memorial sign erected on the westbound lanes of State Route Highway 76, located just west of the Douglas Drive on-ramp, near the OPD. A resolution, championed by assemblywoman Patricia Bates, authorized the tribute to one of Oceanside's fallen officers, designating the four-mile portion of Highway 76 from Douglas Drive to its end at Coast Highway as the "Oceanside Police Officer Tony Zeppetella Memorial Highway." Some police officers starting their shifts out of the station westbound on Highway 76 turn their emergency lights on briefly as they pass the sign, a silent salute to their fallen brother.

Created as a souvenir from a photograph taken in 2003, this postcard depicts an old Oceanside police car that is used as a parade car today. The car was restored by police corporal Matt Lyons and his son Justin. The car, a 1968 Dodge Polara, is pictured parked adjacent to the 101 Café, a historic diner located in Oceanside on Coast Highway. The car bears the number 269, which was the badge number of fallen Ofc. Tony Zeppetella, who was killed in the line of duty on June 13, 2003. (Courtesy Oceanside Police Department Archives.)

le, California
ike going back to a simpler time,
when everything was
Black & White!
OCEANSIDE
POLICE

Motor officer Rich Schickel is pictured here in 2005, sitting on his BMW police edition motorcycle near the Oceanside PD. Officer Schickel, a six-year OPD veteran and former U.S. Marine, had been in the motors section nearly a year at the time of this photograph. His motorcycle is equipped with a helmet mike for his police radio and saddle bags with equipment that allow him to respond to the same calls as officers in traditional police cars. Schickel's motorcycle is equipped with storage compartments that allow him easy access to his handheld radar and laser and his side handle baton as well. (Courtesy Oceanside Police Department Archives.)

With the spirit of Christmas and a sense of brotherhood motivating them, retired police sergeant Tom Bussey and retired police captain Steve Scarano are pictured here in the police department lounge at 3855 Mission Avenue on December 25, 2005, around 5:30 a.m. Both Bussey and Scarano have made this annual pancake breakfast for the changing shifts during countless Christmas holidays. Also pictured is Ofc. Brad Maze, a retired U.S. Marine sergeant major, who appreciates this kind and welcome gesture from these unsung heroes. (Courtesy Oceanside Police Department Archives.)

Ofc. Mark Bussey, hired on December 30, 2003, followed in his brother Matt Bussey and father, Tom Bussey's, footsteps by becoming a police officer with the Oceanside PD. Mark, pictured here in 2003, handled a service call on August 10, 2004, that forever change his life. Mark responded to a report of a forgery suspect at the Bank of America, located across the street from the police department at 3756 Mission Avenue. Officer Bussey arrived and met face-to-face with the suspect, who attempted to flee. Mark gave chase and within moments just outside the bank, the suspect spun around and shot Officer Bussey once in the leg with a small handgun, severely wounding him. The officer fell, but propped himself up in fighting position for a second attack. The suspect kept running and engaging in an open gun battle with Ofc. Mike Brown in the bank parking lot. The suspect was shot dead by responding officers. Officer Bussey recovered from his injuries after six months of rehabilitation and continues to work in the patrol division. (Courtesy Tom Bussey collection.)

Seen in these three 2005 photographs at a training range, located at the nearby Camp Pendleton Marine Corps Base, is the Oceanside Police Department (OPD) SWAT team. The acronym SWAT stands for Special Weapons and Tactics and can be seen on the team's black-and-white van. These officers are specially trained to work as a team during critical incidents and receive advanced weapons and tactics training before being assigned to the specialized duties. Selection to the OPD SWAT team is a competitive and rigorous process, and only the best officers are selected for this elite duty. SWAT members must be able to respond at a moment's notice from anywhere in the San Diego County area to the location of a critical incident. (Courtesy Oceanside Police Department Archives.)

Five

Police Facilities, Uniforms, Insignia, and Equipment

The original city hall building, pictured here in 1888 on Hill and Second Streets, held the original city marshal office, located on the second floor. Although this building no longer exists, Marshal C. C. Wilson worked alongside his younger brother J. Keno Wilson here. (Courtesy Oceanside Historical Society.)

The badge can be one of the most important tools that detectives have, because it is one of the only clearly recognizable pieces of equipment identifying them as law enforcement. The title of detective is reserved for an elite group of investigative professionals, earned after a competitive selection and years of proving oneself on the streets as a uniformed officer. This badge was used during the 1980s and would be considered a series-three Oceanside-style badge, as it has an eagle on the top, unlike others worn by Oceanside police. (Courtesy Oceanside Police Department Archives.)

Looking for trace evidence requires a lot of patience and a good eye. At night, that job can be even more challenging. This 1984 photograph features Ofc. Paul Simpson using a high-powered light designed especially for this task. (Courtesy Oceanside Police Department Archives.)

The briefing room is where most police departments share and exchange information, passing on intelligence from one shift to another. This 1984 photograph shows officers and detectives being briefed by the shift sergeant at the old police station, located at 1617 Mission Avenue. (Courtesy Oceanside Police Department Archives.)

Oceanside PD, like many large departments, must deal with problems that require the use of a helicopter. Pictured here during the 1990s, an Oceanside helicopter lifts off to provide cover for another officer. This air program was very effective, but it was eventually scrapped when it became cost prohibitive. Today Oceanside contracts with the San Diego County Sheriff's Department for air support. (Courtesy Oceanside Police Department Archives.)

Patrolling the Oceanside beach, officers had more mobility using this 1980s Jeep Cherokee outfitted with full-emergency equipment. The jeep allowed officers to drive onto the beach and address problems quickly without worrying about getting stuck. (Courtesy Oceanside Police Department Archives.)

This photograph, taken during the 1990s next to the Oceanside Pier, shows a Jeep CJ-7 and Quad ATV outfitted and marked as police vehicles. Both vehicles provided increased mobility on the busy Oceanside beach. Standing next to the vehicle is a non-sworn beach security officer used to handle minor problems that did not require a sworn police officer. (Courtesy Oceanside Police Department Archives.)

During the 1970s, officers are training in felony high-risk traffic stops. The unmarked detective car being stopped is a 1968, four-door Dodge Polara, used both by detectives and patrol at one point. The white marked car is an early 1970s AMC Matador outfitted with a red rotating emergency light, interior cage, and adjustable spotlight on the roof. (Courtesy Oceanside Police Department Archives.)

In 1991, this is the Oceanside Communications and Dispatch Center for the police department at the station located at 1617 Mission Avenue. Two televisions, mounted on brackets above the dispatchers' heads, monitored the front desk and entrance via closed-circuit video. (Courtesy Oceanside Police Department Archives.)

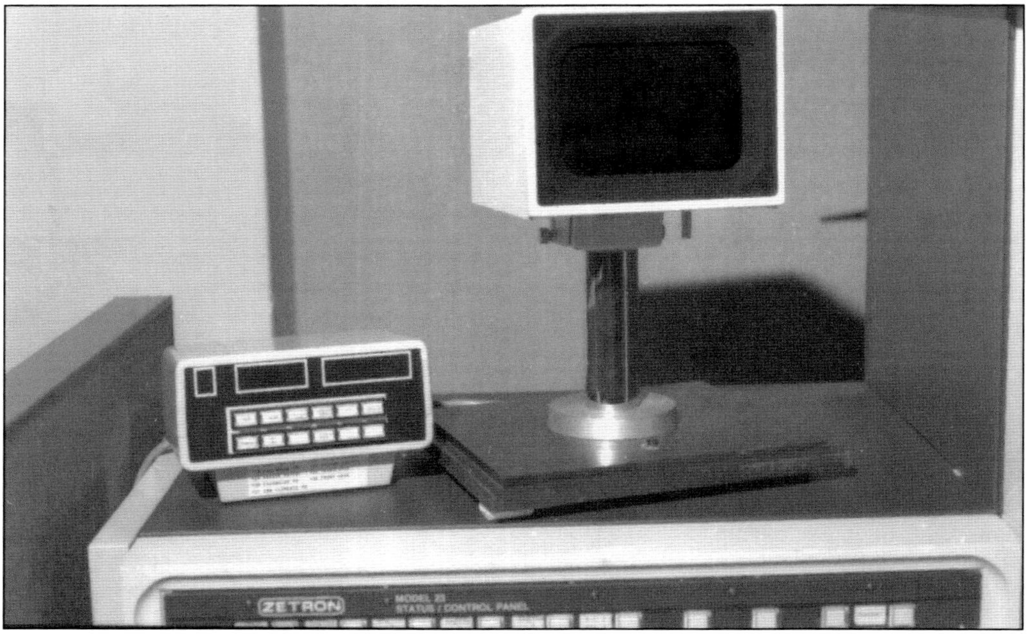

Developed in the 1990s, the 911 system speeds up services and increases emergency service response times. The early 911 monitor that Oceanside dispatchers had to use seems primitive compared to today's technology; however, it was state of the art and very efficient for its time. (Courtesy Oceanside Police Department Archives.)

In this photograph, an Oceanside 911 dispatcher completes a call for a service card that will be radioed to a mobile patrol car. During the early 1990s, dispatchers wore a light blue shirt with a police department patch. Today police dispatchers wear a pullover, collared shirt with an embroidered logo on the front. There are no patches. (Courtesy Oceanside Police Department Archives.)

During the 1960s, the police department dealt with a lot of protestors due to the unpopular Vietnam War. Officers during this period were required to wear safety helmets. The helmet pictured here was issued during the late 1970s and had an attached clear face shield to protect from debris and objects being thrown in the officer's face. (Courtesy Matthew J. Lyons.)

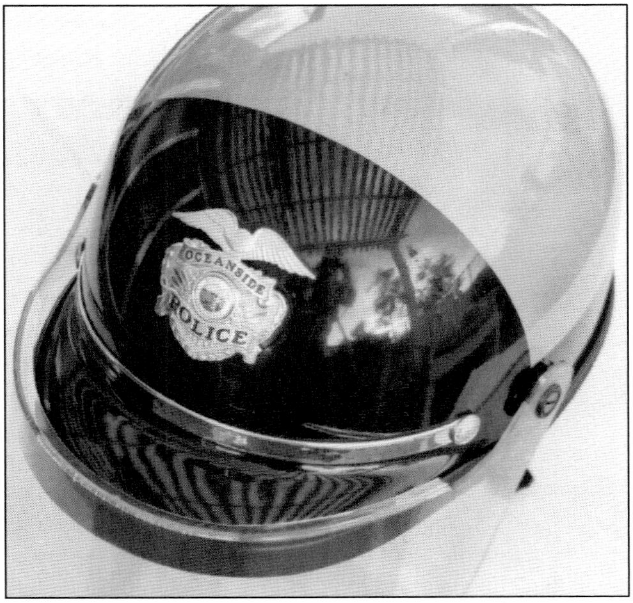

In 2005, this helmet, known as a riot helmet, was issued to police officers in Oceanside. It closely resembles those issued to military personnel. This helmet has a clear face shield to protect the officer's face. Officers are required to have this helmet with them at all times while on duty. (Courtesy Oceanside Police Department Archives.)

California winters aren't very cold, unless you are riding a police motorcycle in the dead of night. These gloves were worn by Capt. Harold B. Davis in the 1930s. They provided warmth from the harsh winds and protection should the rider fall to the ground. (Courtesy Capt. H. B. Davis family.)

In 1934, Oceanside became the fifth police department in the nation to install police radios in their patrol cars. This is the original radio and speaker used in Capt. H. B. Davis's car. The radio was not always reliable. While it would sometimes work, there were other times it was of no use at all. (Courtesy Capt. H. B. Davis family.)

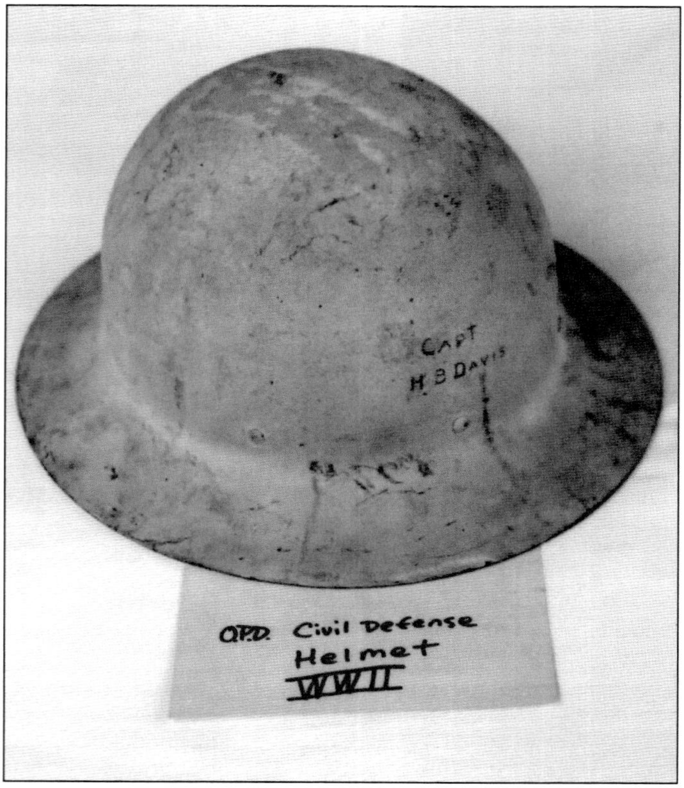

Early police reserve officers wore a white military-style helmet, like this one worn by Capt. H. B. Davis. Reserve civil defense officers were used during World War II and paired up with uniformed officers. (Courtesy Capt. H. B. Davis family.)

This police officer's hat is called a Pershing, or LAPD-style hat. Oceanside police officers wore this hat from 1982 until the 1990s, when the style was changed to the Smokey Bear–style. (Courtesy Oceanside Police Department Archives.)

This hat is called a campaign-style or Mounties-style hat. Although not worn often and not very popular with officers, it was adopted for wear during the 1990s, when it was determined that this hat would offer better protection from the sun's harmful rays. (Courtesy Oceanside Police Department Archives.)

These patches were worn by Capt. H. B. Davis during the 1930s and 1940s. The top is an armband for police reserves that augmented the regular officers. The two patches with winged wheels and arrows were used to designate a motor officer and worn on each sleeve near the bicep. The patch reading "Police Traffic" designated a traffic accident investigator. The star was worn on the shirt near the left cuff and represented five years of service, while each hash mark represents one year of service. (i.e., two stars and three hash marks represented 13 years of service.) (Courtesy Capt. H. B. Davis family.)

This series-three Oceanside eagle top badge No. 5 was one of the early badges used during the 1930s by Capt. H. B. Davis when he was first hired by the police department. A simple clutch pin-style device was used to fasten it to the shirt. (Courtesy Capt. H. B. Davis family.)

These two hat badges were used by Capt. Davis during his 25-year career from the 1930s to 1955. The one on the left was for regular full-time officers, while the one on the right was used by reserve police officers, who only worked part-time. The badges had two screw posts on the back used to fasten them to the hat itself. (Courtesy Capt. H. B. Davis family.)

This hat was worn by Capt. H. B. Davis from the 1930s until 1950, when the color of the uniforms changed to tan. This blue hat had a gold band and simple gold "P" screw post to fasten the band to the hat. (Courtesy Capt. H. B. Davis family.)

This patch is the only patch ever used by the Oceanside Police Department and was first used in 1940s. The patch is white in color with blue lettering and the city seal in the center. The city seal is divided into quarters depicting the connection to the Mission San Luis Rey; a bear, which is the state symbol; a fish to symbolize the fishing industry, and a cornucopia to symbolize the bounty that Oceanside has to offer. (Courtesy Oceanside Police Department Archives.)

This hat was worn by Capt. H. B. Davis from 1950 until his retirement in 1955. The tan uniforms and hats had become very popular in California and many departments adopted the style. This hat like the blue one had a gold hat band and simple gold "P" screw post to fasten the band to the hat. Oceanside would continue to wear the tan uniform and hat until 1982, when they changed back to the blue uniform. (Courtesy Capt. H. B. Davis family.)

This gold-filled chief's badge was presented to Capt. H. B. Davis in recognition of his years of service and the numerous occasions he filled in as acting police chief. The front of the badge had a ruby stone in the eagle's eye and four diamond stones on the four stars. The back of the badge shows the inscription presented to Davis upon his retirement, "May 13, 1930. Harold B. Davis Retired Oceanside Police 6-30-55." (Courtesy Capt. H. B. Davis family.)

This Royal typewriter was used during the 1930s and 1940s at the Oceanside Police Department on 305 North Nevada Street to write reports and correspondence. While today's computer word processors allow an officer to clear up a mistake on a report with a simple keystroke, officers of that time had to start all over to correct their mistakes. (Courtesy Capt. H. B. Davis family.)

These two flashlights were used by Capt. H. B. Davis while he patrolled the streets of Oceanside during the 1930s and 1940s. His name was inscribed on both flashlights to identify them as his property. (Courtesy Capt. H. B. Davis family.)

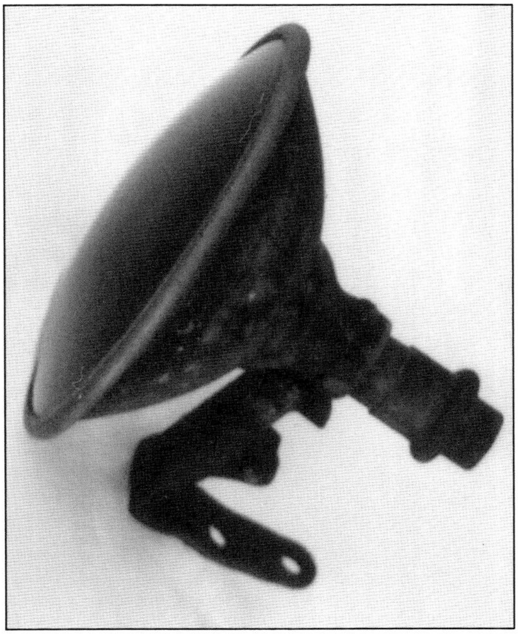

The California vehicle code requires that all emergency vehicles be equipped with one solid red light. Today all California emergency vehicles have that one red light that remains on while others flash or rotate. During the 1930s, Capt. H. B. Davis had this single red light as his only emergency-vehicle identification. The light was mounted on the police car's left front fender so citizens would know to stop or pull over. My, how technology has improved! (Courtesy Capt. H. B. Davis family.)

During World War II, cars had to be equipped with a blackout light, which reduced the amount of light created at night by traditional car headlights. This light, a simple tube with a small pinhole at the end to allow light to pass through, was used by the Oceanside Police Department on the police cars in the 1940s. Two of these lights were mounted on the fenders and would provide just enough light to mark the road traveled on. (Courtesy Capt. H. B. Davis family.)

This photograph of a 1939 Plymouth was taken during the Fourth of July parade in 1941, while Ofc. H. B. Davis and Chief Warren Paxton rode in the parade. Officer Davis noted the car only lasted nine months from the time they got it used. (Courtesy Capt. H. B. Davis family.)

In 1939, the local Shell station offered free brake checks. Here Chief Warren Paxton is getting the brakes on this 1936 Ford checked. (Courtesy Capt. H. B. Davis family.)

Ofcs. Harold Davis and Leon Emo sit aboard an Oceanside police Harley Davidson in 1943, near Officer Davis's home in Oceanside, California. (Courtesy Capt. H. B. Davis family.)

Oceanside was credited as being the fifth police department in the nation to have a police car radio in 1935. Pictured here next to his 1940 Ford coupe is Ofc. H. B. Davis using that radio. (Courtesy Capt. H. B. Davis family.)

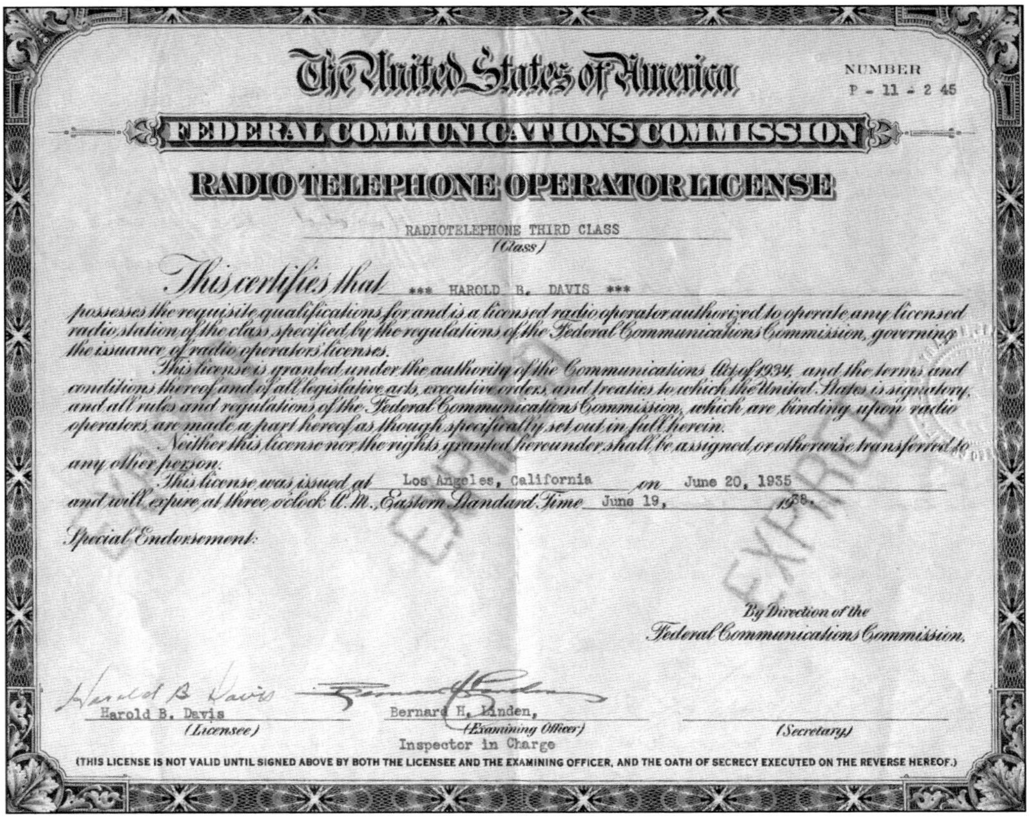

The United States of America

NUMBER P-11-2 45

FEDERAL COMMUNICATIONS COMMISSION

RADIO TELEPHONE OPERATOR LICENSE

RADIOTELEPHONE THIRD CLASS
(Class)

This certifies that *** HAROLD B. DAVIS ***
possesses the requisite qualifications for and is a licensed radio operator authorized to operate any licensed radio station of the class specified by the regulations of the Federal Communications Commission, governing the issuance of radio operators' licenses.

This license is granted under the authority of the Communications Act of 1934, and the terms and conditions thereof and of all legislative acts, executive orders, and treaties to which the United States is signatory, and all rules and regulations of the Federal Communications Commission, which are binding upon radio operators, are made a part hereof as though specifically set out in full herein.

Neither this license nor the rights granted hereunder shall be assigned, or otherwise transferred to any other person.

This license was issued at Los Angeles, California on June 20, 1935 and will expire at three o'clock A.M., Eastern Standard Time June 19, 1938.

Special Endorsement:

EXPIRED EXPIRED

By Direction of the
Federal Communications Commission.

Harold B. Davis (Licensee) — Bernard H. Linden, (Examining Officer) Inspector in Charge — (Secretary)

(THIS LICENSE IS NOT VALID UNTIL SIGNED ABOVE BY BOTH THE LICENSEE AND THE EXAMINING OFFICER, AND THE OATH OF SECRECY EXECUTED ON THE REVERSE HEREOF.)

During the 1930s, this certificate was issued to Ofc. H. B. Davis after he passed a written exam proving he could use the new police radios in the cars and at the station. Davis had to travel to Los Angeles to take the training. (Courtesy Capt. H. B. Davis family.)

This photograph depicts the first radio room of the police station at 305 North Nevada Street. The call letters for the police department were KADI. This was state-of-the-art technology for its time. (Courtesy Capt. H. B. Davis family.)

This photograph depicts the first update to the radio room shortly after the department had begun using the radio-to-car system in the late 1930s. The call letters remained KADI. (Courtesy Capt. H. B. Davis family.)

This early 1940s photograph shows Ofcs. H. B. Davis and Guy Woodard standing next to a 1941 Plymouth near Officer Woodard's home in Oceanside, California. (Courtesy Capt. H. B. Davis family.)

During the 1970s, an unidentified police matron/meter maid stands in uniform next to a 1970s Cushman police vehicle in the parking of the police station at 1617 Mission Avenue. (Courtesy Oceanside Police Department Archives.)

Behind the Oceanside police station at 1617 Mission Avenue is a 1970s Chevrolet Impala squad car. The department had recently begun installing cages, separating the front and back seats. (Courtesy Oceanside Police Department Archives.)

The communication center was located at 1617 Mission Avenue. Each dispatcher was separated by a half wall and had television monitors positioned towards them. (Courtesy Oceanside Police Department Archives.)

Pictured in this 1980s photograph is the front of the Oceanside police station that opened in 1968 under the leadership of Chief Ward Ratcliff. The police department would remain at that location until 1997, when it moved to Mission Avenue and El Camino Real. (Courtesy Oceanside Police Department Archives.)

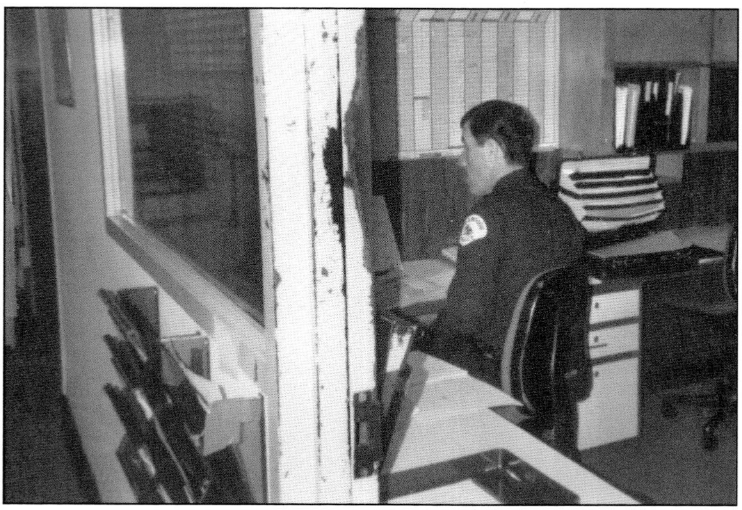

In the 1980s, Ofc. Frank Bruckner sits in the watch commander's office at the police station, located at 1617 Mission Avenue. This facility quickly grew small, outdated, and worn with the high volume of traffic through it. (Courtesy Oceanside Police Department Archives.)

This photograph taken during the 1980s shows the reel-to-reel communications system used by the police department at the police station at 1617 Mission Avenue. Today a dispatcher will record radio transmission through digital recordings. (Courtesy Oceanside Police Department Archives.)

This 2005 Ford Crown Victoria was used as a police car. Officers now have a computer terminal inside their cab interior and can run checks on subjects from the field, without the assistance of a dispatcher. (Courtesy Oceanside Police Department Archives.)

During the 1960s and 1970s, this patch was worn on the shoulders of the dispatcher's shirt. Today dispatchers wear a more casual collared pullover shirt with embroidery on the front for ease and comfort. (Courtesy Oceanside Police Department Archives.)

This patch was worn on the sleeves of police officers during the 1970s and 1980s to designate them as K-9 officers. Today's K-9 officers wear a small patch pin with a canine above the nametag. (Courtesy Oceanside Police Department Archives.)

This pin, although not official wear, was created when a dispatch center was formed at the Special Enforcement Division while the communication center at 1617 Mission Avenue was being updated in the 1980s. (Courtesy Oceanside Police Department Archives.)

The Oceanside PD's Medal of Valor is considered the highest award an officer can receive and may be awarded to members who distinguished themselves by an act of heroism, performing at the risk of grave personal injury or death. (Courtesy Oceanside Police Department Archives.)

The Oceanside PD's Purple Heart may be awarded to members who are seriously wounded or killed as result of a hostile or life-threatening encounter. (Courtesy Oceanside Police Department Archives.)

The Oceanside PD's Life Saving Medal may be awarded to members who distinguish themselves by performing an extraordinary act that saves human life that otherwise would have resulted in death. (Courtesy Oceanside Police Department Archives.)

The Oceanside PD's Distinguished Service Medal may be awarded to members for exceptional achievement in assigned duties with loyalty and dedication over a prolonged period of time. (Courtesy Oceanside Police Department Archives.)

The Oceanside PD's Medal of Merit may be awarded to members who perform superior accomplishments that result in significant contribution to the efficient operation of the department. (Courtesy Oceanside Police Department Archives.)

Buddy Devine was an ambulance driver, with badge and gun, in the 1930s. From the early 1930s to the late 1970s, the police department was responsible for all ambulance operations. Ambulance drivers often had limited authority, and some wore sidearms and badges. (Courtesy Oceanside Historical Society.)

Here is a special Oceanside police badge dating to the 1930s. It is similar to the one pictured above. (Courtesy police historian Nathan Semel.)

This Oceanside police sergeant badge dates to the 1930s. (Courtesy Police Historian Nathan Semel.)

This 1940s Oceanside police sergeant badge was made of steel. (Courtesy Police Historian Nathan Semel.)

This Oceanside consultant's badge dates to the 1970s. (Courtesy Oceanside Police.)

This photograph shows a 1960s Oceanside reserve policewoman's badge. (Courtesy Oceanside Police.)

Six

OCEANSIDE HARBOR DISTRICT POLICE DEPARTMENT

The Oceanside Harbor District Police Department is a separate police department from the Oceanside Police Department and was formed in 1963. Pictured in this 1980s photograph is harbor police officer Pete Munoz, who is operating a 29-foot Crystal Liner rescue boat. This boat is equipped with firefighting equipment and turnout gear, as well as scuba gear. (Courtesy Oceanside Harbor District Police Department archives.)

This patch is the second one used by the Oceanside Harbor District Police Department. Blue with gold lettering, it reads "Harbor Police," with the harbor district seal in the center. The first patch used by the Harbor District Police Department was similar to this design; however, it was gold in color, with blue lettering and read "Harbor Patrol." The second patch would change again in the 1990s. (Courtesy Oceanside Harbor District Police Department archives.)

At the time the Oceanside Harbor District Police Department was created in the 1960s, this was the police officer's badge. The department changed badges in 1997 when the Oceanside Police Department changed theirs. (Courtesy Police Historian Nathan Semel.)

During the 1960s, this Oceanside Harbor District police officer works a recruiting and public relations display. The harbor district was created in Oceanside in 1961 and its police department was formed in 1963 as part of the bond agreement. Harbor officers are sworn California police officers with the same authority as defined in the California Penal Code. (Courtesy Oceanside Harbor District Police Department archives.)

The Oceanside Pier is used for recreation from sunup to sundown. Some poor souls end it all by jumping off the pier; some accidentally fall. Here, in 1980, Oceanside Harbor District police officers and city police officers attempt a rescue of one of those souls in rough waters. (Courtesy Oceanside Harbor District Police Department archives.)

Oceanside Harbor District Police officers inspect a UFO as it comes into the Oceanside Harbor in the 1960s. This vessel, made to look like a flying saucer, was a prop used in the production of a science fiction film. It was towed into the Oceanside Harbor for a publicity photograph shoot, and harbor officers inspected it before allowing it to dock. (Courtesy Oceanside Harbor District Police Department archives.)

This 1983 photograph, with the Oceanside Harbor in the background, shows a blue Chevrolet Blazer outfitted with a push bumper, spotlights, emergency lights, and a cage to separate the driver from the rear seating area for prisoners. (Courtesy Oceanside Harbor District Police Department archives.)

The Oceanside Harbor District police are sworn officers who must be trained in law enforcement and rescue techniques. Here, in the 1980s, two harbor officers are aboard their marked red police boat, located at the mouth of the Oceanside Harbor. (Courtesy Oceanside Harbor District Police Department archives.)

Pictured in the 1960s in front of the Harbor District Office/Harbor District Police Department, the harbormaster and officers in the newly formed Harbor Police Department pose proudly. (Courtesy Oceanside Harbor District Police Department archives.)

This 1970s photograph offers a view of the Oceanside Harbor District headquarters. This building also houses the Harbor District Police Department. Officers use this building for report writing and other administrative tasks; however, they are supported by the city police department for the dispatching and booking of prisoners. (Courtesy Oceanside Harbor District Police Department archives.)

This 1970s photograph was taken from the vantage point of a harbor officer looking over the bow of the police boat returning into the harbor. The "Oceanside" sign is reminiscent of the larger, more famous "Hollywood" sign. (Courtesy Oceanside Harbor District Police Department archives.)

Chiefs of the Oceanside Police Department

Charles Goss	1925–1934
Ernest Henry	1934–1936
Warren Paxton	1936–1944
William Coyle	1944–1947
Guy Woodward	1947–1950
Roger Gates	1950–1952
Edwin Patrick	1952–1955
Forrest Duke	1955–1955
William Wingard	1955–1962
Ward Ratcliff	1962–1975
Rolf Henze	1975–1981
Laurence Marshall	1981–1987
Robert Smith	1987–1988
Oliver Drummond	1989–1990
R. Bruce Dunne	1991–1995
Michael Poehlman	1995–2005
Jerome Lance	2005–2006
Frank McCoy	2006–present

Oceanside Police Department Line of Duty Deaths

Charles Clinton Wilson
End of Watch July 4, 1889
killed by gunfire

John Mugan
End of Watch September 24, 1916
killed by gunfire

Tony W. Zeppetella
End of Watch June 13, 2003
killed by gunfire